The
CRYSTAL
HANDBOOK

The
CRYSTAL
HANDBOOK

Denise Whichello Brown & Judith Millidge

© 2007 D&S Books Ltd

© 2009 Kerswell Farm Ltd

This edition published by Kerswell Books Ltd

Printed 2009

This book is distributed in the UK by

Parkham Books Ltd

Kerswell Farm,

Parkham Ash, Bideford

Devon, England

EX39 5PR

enquiries@parkhambooks.co.uk

ISBN: 978-1-906239-28-2

DS0148. Crystal Handbook

Creative Director: Sarah King

Project editor: Claire Bone

Designer: Debbie Fisher & Co

Material in this book previously appeared in *The Power of Crystals*

Printed in Singapore

1 3 5 7 9 10 8 6 4 2

CONTENTS

INTRODUCTION

Mention crystals, and many people imagine beautiful, faceted, sparkling stones that dazzle onlookers – and indeed countless highly prized crystal gems are like that. But even in their natural state, crystals that emerge from the rough, dull rocks around them have a strange, natural beauty, which has meant that since time immemorial humankind has subscribed special powers to them. Quartz, which is the basis of so many crystals, is the most common mineral in the earth's crust, and the piercing colours of many gemstones are simply the result of impurities that seep into that mineral during its formation underground. The word crystal is often used simply to describe shiny, cut stones, but in scientific terms, a crystalline structure describes the internal arrangement of the molecular or atomic particles of a material. Many materials have crystalline structures – all metals, for example, and a great number of minerals. Furthermore, crystals can easily be grown in a laboratory.

O·Quartz is the most common mineral in the earth's crust – and the basis of many crystals

For the purposes of this book, we shall use the word crystal to describe a stone that has become valued for its rarity, beauty or healing powers. Some of the stones used in crystal healing are not crystals at all: amber, for example, used for thousands of years in healing and jewellery-making, is actually fossilised resin from coniferous trees and is classified as a mineraloid. The word crystal comes from the Greek, krystallos, meaning ice. The ancient Greeks believed that rock crystal was water that had been frozen forever by the gods, and it was not until 1784 that the French mineralogist René-Just Haüy (1743–1822) dropped one and discovered that, under magnification, the fragments all displayed a similar appearance. He published his theory on the structure of crystals shortly after and paved the way for our modern understanding of mineral forms and crystallography.

○·The Ancient Greeks believed crystals were water frozen by the Gods.

8

For thousands of years, peoples all over the world have attributed mystical powers to crystals. Drawn by the beauty of the stones, they have used them to foretell the future, cure ailments and protect themselves from harm. Sceptics may dismiss crystal therapy as tosh, but the physical attributes of crystals, such as the piezoelectric properties of quartz, mean that crystals can harness powers, some of which are still beyond so-called rational explanation.

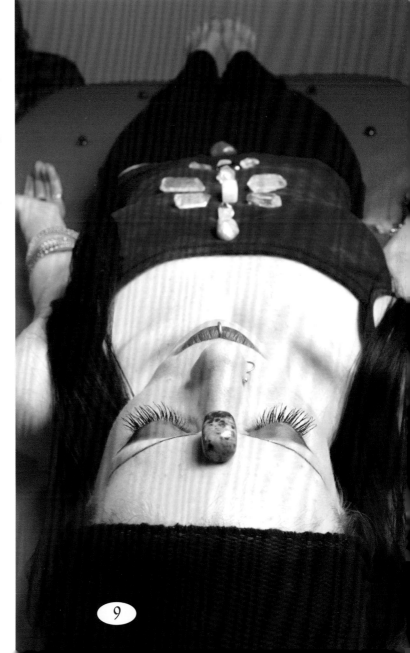

○·The healing power of crystals has been a popular belief for centuries.

9

ABOUT CRYSTALS

Although crystals and gems have never really lost their popularity, the recent interest in 'new age' therapies has meant that growing numbers of people have acquired a knowledge of the healing power of crystals. The pages that follow provide a guide to choosing crystals and how to use them to enhance your health and well being. Finally, there is a guide to over 50 different crystals, noting their physical properties, their historical and legendary uses, and the best way to use them as part of crystal therapy.

THE GEOLOGY AND MINERALOGY OF CRYSTALS

The formation of minerals

Rocks are composed of mixtures of different minerals, and minerals themselves are described as naturally occurring substances with a defined chemical composition that usually possess a crystalline structure. Minerals are identified by the structure of their crystalline system, by their colour, hardness on the Mohs scale (see page 132), lustre, density, cleavage and fracture. With over 4,000 minerals on Earth, they form in a wide variety of different environments. However, the earth is dominated by some 30 common minerals, and the rest present themselves as traces in rocks; concentrations of trace minerals are the source of materials like ores from which metals are extracted. Minerals are formed in four main ways.

1. Hot molten magma cools and then crystallizes

2. Chemicals dissolve in water

3. Existing minerals react with their environment and alter chemically, e.g. oxidization

4. Minerals are subject to intense heat or pressure which alters their chemical structure

Minerals crystallize into geometric shapes that vary according to their symmetry and structure. There are six main crystal groups or systems used to describe the internal molecular arrangement of minerals:

Cubic

Tetragonal

Monoclinic

Triclinic

Hexagonal/triagonal

Orthorhombic

Crystals grow in cracks in rocks, often squeezed on all sides by the immense pressure of other rocks, so they never achieve a perfect outer form in nature. Their internal structure, however, is part of what defines them. It is symmetrical in some way and conforms to the Law of Constancy of Angle, which states that the angle between the faces of a particular mineral is always the same, and this is one way in which geologists identify them.

O·Here you can see a band of quartz within a sandstone rock. South Australia

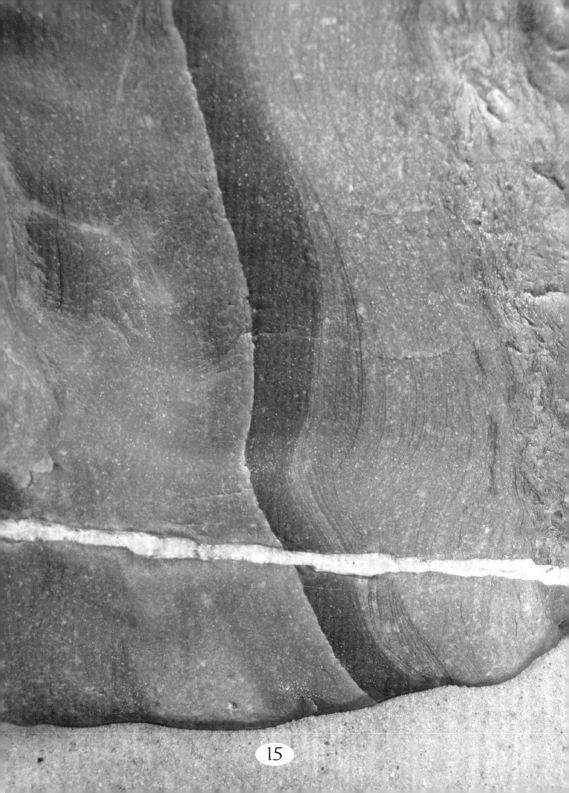

Sizes range from tiny gems to spectacular long structures up to 20 ft long. In 2001 the largest natural crystals ever found were discovered in a silver and zinc mine in Chihuahua, Mexico. Beautiful selenite crystals over 20 ft (6 metres) in length were discovered in two caves which themselves are the size of small houses, 1,200 ft (365 metres) below the surface. Mexican officials hope to keep the crystals in their natural habitat and open the caves to the public, but are hampered by the extreme heat and humidity of the site.

The physical properties of minerals, and therefore, crystals are assessed by examining hardness, how they bend or break (cleavage, fracture and tenacity) the specific gravity, and their reaction to acid. Looks are important, too and it is easy to identify some stones simply from their shape or colour. More tricky rocks are assessed for their colour – both externally and from their 'streak' (the colour of their powdered form). The lustre, whether the surface is shiny or dull, is considered on a ten-point scale ranging from adamantine (brilliant and shiny like a diamond) to dull. The way they reflect or refract light is also important. Transparent minerals include clear quartz; translucent crystals such as aquamarine allow light to pass through; and opaque specimens, such as jade, do not. Fluorescence – the glow of the stone in ultraviolet light – is also measured. (For further details see p130 at the beginning of the A–Z section.)

Facing page: Natural amethyst topped by quartz crystal peaks.

GEMSTONES

How do we define a gemstone? After all, it's just another shiny bit of mineral lodged in rock, and many of the world's most prized gems look rather ordinary before they are cut and polished. In the past, colour was probably the most immediate prized feature – and the more vivid the better. For dealers and jewellers today, gems are assessed with the four Cs: clarity, cut, colour and carat.

O The vivid colours shown in this rough piece of Tiger Iron from Western Australia, are transformed when the minerals and gemstones are polished.

There are only 130 minerals which are regarded as gemstones, and of them, only 50 are in regular use. Formed in uncommon geological conditions, gemstones are rare treasures in a world of dull rock, hence their immense value. The four most valuable are diamond, emerald (green beryl) ruby (red conundrum) and sapphire (blue conundrum). The remainder – fabulous crystals such as aquamarine, lapis lazuli, topaz, opal or jade – are classified as semi-precious stones.

THE MOST VALUABLE GEMSTONES

Diamond

Emerald

Ruby

Sapphire

Before the middle ages the great majority of precious stones were simply polished along their natural breaks, so the stones used in the jewels of royalty and the nobility would not have had the fabulous cuts and facets of today's gems. One of the earliest method of polishing diamonds was discovered in 1456 by Louis Berquen of Bruges. It was not until about 1700 that the technology emerged to enable jewellers to shape gemstones and they realised that gemstones could be cut or ground into specific shapes to produce faceted gems whose beauty literally sparkled in the faces of those who gazed upon them. Over the centuries jewellers found different styles of cutting suited different stones: hard gems like diamonds and rubies benefited from multiple triangular cuts to make them glitter and reflect the light, while opaque or translucent stones like opal or lapis lazuli looked better cut en cabochon, with a rounded top.

○ Different styles of gem-set jewellery

CRYSTALS IN HISTORY

Evidence from Palaeolithic times suggests that rocks were the first objects used as religious idols by humankind. Stones were mankind's first tools, weapons, and, in the form of caves, shelters. Stones and rocks protected people and kept them alive, so from the stone circles of the European druids, to the monumental stone images on Easter Island in the Pacific Ocean, it is not surprising that they associated them with their gods. As people became nomadic, there is evidence that they carried with them stones and rocks from their tribe's place of origin, and these stones – tangible reminders of their homeland – became very precious to them.

O In ancient times rocks had religious significance – such as Stonehenge.]

Crystals are attractive on a very basic level – unlike the dull grey stones in which they are often found, crystals are colourful and reflect the light – so they became precious and were used by the rulers of society to enhance their status. The Aboriginal peoples of Australia believed that opals appeared on earth at the spot where God put his feet when he came down to earth on a rainbow to spread a message of peace and love. The ancient Greeks classified stones according to their colour and attributed male characteristics to dark stones, and female attributes to lighter ones. Precious stones and crystals became part of their folklore and legends. They believed that yellow topaz was a stone of strength associated with the sun, and that it could render the wearer invisible in time of trouble. Amethyst, for example, was regarded as a stone that would prevent drunkenness, so goblets were often made from it, and hardened drinkers often wore amethyst amulets to stave off intoxication and presumably, hangovers.

O Crystals come in a range of colours and textures

In China, jade 'the essence of heaven and earth', was regarded as the most precious natural material and was revered as an extremely powerful stone. It was inserted into the ears of the dead and another piece was put into their hands in the belief that it would preserve the body from decay. Powdered jade was often mixed with honey and milk and given to nursing mothers to improve the flow of their milk.

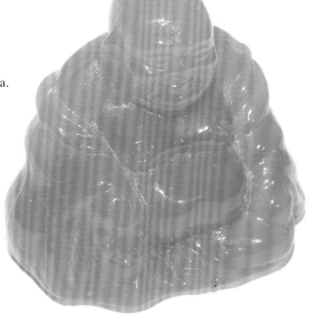

O Jade was considered the most precious stone in Ancient China.

The Chinese used colour to attribute value to their gems and this is illustrated by the badges of rank worn by the court officials – the higher the status of the office holder, the better his rank badge. Mandarins of the first rank wore red stones such as ruby or pink tourmaline; the next step down in the hierarchy wore coral and garnet, while blue stones such as lapis lazuli or aquamarine designated third rank bureaucrats. Rock crystal was worn by those of the fourth rank, and other white stones by officials of the fifth rank.

In the Bible, when God commanded Moses to lead his people out of Egypt, he also gave detailed instructions about the style in which they should worship Him once they had reached the Promised Land. In Exodus (28:15-21) there is a thorough description of the jewelled breastplate that was to be worn by the Jewish high priest:

> 'Fashion a breastpiece for making decisions—the work of a skilled craftsman. Make it like the ephod: of gold, and of blue, purple and scarlet yarn, and of finely twisted linen. It is to be square—a span [a] long and a span wide—and folded double. Then mount four rows of precious stones on it. In the first row there shall be a ruby, a topaz and a beryl; in the second row a turquoise, a sapphire and an emerald; in the third row a jacinth, an agate and an amethyst; in the fourth row a chrysolite, an onyx and a jasper. Mount them in gold filigree settings. There are to be twelve stones, one for each of the names of the sons of Israel, each engraved like a seal with the name of one of the twelve tribes.'

The stones chosen were highly valued, either for their rarity or beauty, or for the healing powers attributed to them. Various legends have sprung up around the stones used in the breastplate, but the truth is that over the passage of time and with the many challenges inherent in Biblical translation, we will never be exactly sure precisely which stones were used. The Hebrews acquired their precious stones from Arabia, Egypt and India, and each one in the breastplate came to represent one of the twelve tribes of Israel, named after the sons of Jacob. In Biblical times stones were named according to their place of origin or colour, rather than being classified by their composition or crystalline forms, and the names of some stones have simply changed: the Biblical sapphire is what we call lapis lazuli, and chrysolite is what we call topaz, which was worn to drive away devils and other fears of the night. Jacinth is a red variety of zircon and was believed to protect the wearer against storms and tempests. Other stones, such as emerald, for example, are unmistakeable; a sparkling deep green, emerald apparently had the power to preserve or heal sight.

○ In Biblical times the stone we know as Lapis Lazuli was known as a sapphire.

O In Ancient Egypt, lapis lazuli was considered a sacred stone

In the same period the ancient Egyptians also used precious stones and crystals as part of their ceremonial and for them, colour was of paramount symbolic importance. Lapis lazuli, the colour of the sky and heaven, was regarded as a royal stone and widely used in the headdresses of the pharaohs. Green malachite, which symbolised life, was also incorporated into headgear as it was regarded as an aid to wise judgement. Red was

usually associated with blood, with all its connotations of energy, power and the life force itself. Red carnelian was placed with the dead to ease their passage into the afterlife and haematite was worn as an amulet to guard against stomach complaints. Funerary jewellery was an important part of the ritual surrounding death, and the Book of the Dead laid down precise instructions for the adornment of the corpse. An amulet made of red jasper had to be placed at the throat of the mummy because the red colouring emphasised the words of the spell,

'You have your blood, Isis; you have your power.'

O In Ancient Rome, green malachite was associated with the mother goddess, Venus.

27

Like the ancient Egyptians, the Romans believed that colours of various stones were symbolically important. Malachite became associated with Venus, the mother of the gods, so green malachite became associated with childbirth and acquired the power to lessen the pains of menstruation or labour. Interestingly, the Vikings made the same link, and greens stones became sacred to Freya, their mother goddess. The red flecks of haematite were associated with blood, and soldiers often carried it as an amulet to protect them on the battlefield. Perhaps as a continuance of the Greek belief that quartz was ice permanently frozen by the gods, the Romans carried clear quartz crystals to keep them cool during the hot summer months. Carnelian (also known as sardius in ancient Rome) was associated with justice and was used to make beautifully carved signet rings. Emerald was believed to alleviate eye problems and the Emperor Nero was an early adopter of sunglasses when he watched gladiatorial contests through a couple of emeralds. According to Pliny, Roman doctors used clear quartz crystal to focus the rays of the sun to cauterise wounds. Amber was worn as an amulet and had medicinal powers to cure fevers when ground up with honey, though as Pliny drily remarks, 'it is not for this reason that the women are so pleased with it' – it was also worked into beautiful jewellery. Diamond had the power to neutralise poisons, banish delirium and to calm the mind – Romans used it boost courage.

O During medieval times, crystals were believed to hold incredible powers – as well as protecting against ailments, witchcraft and ill-feeling. For example Topaz could render the wearer invisible!

29

Pliny the Elder's magisterial work Naturalis Historia not only records the Roman beliefs regarding a great many gems and crystals, but his ideas were passed down the generations and his pronouncements were often accepted without question at least until the Renaissance. So in medieval times, it was commonly believed that coral cured madness, that sapphire offered protection against envy, and that chrysoprase would protect a thief from hanging. In an age of superstition, crystals were used to treat every ailment that might befall the human body, and many others beside. Protection against witchcraft was almost as valuable as preventing the occurrence of the many life-threatening afflictions that were so prevalent. Topaz could apparently render the wearer invisible, turquoise was reputed to change colour if the wearer was becoming ill, and widows were advised to wear garnets to help them acquire a new husband.

○ Facing page: The Aztecs used obsidian swords and spears as weapons, rather than metal.

31

Lacking the technological knowledge to forge metal, the Aztecs used obsidian as a lethal weapon – to the surprise of the Spanish Conquistadors, who carried state of the art 16th century military armour – early firearms and sharpened swords. The Aztecs also polished obsidian (as the Romans and Greeks did) and used is as mirror both in ritual and practical ways. They also venerated jade and linked it to the rain god Ilaloi, who had the power of life and death. When the Spaniards came across it, they called it pedras de ijada (stone of the side) because the Aztecs told them it would cure kidney complaints. The Native Americans prized turquoise, because they believed that it linked heaven and earth (and the Tibetans held a similar belief).

○ Turquoise was prized by the Native Americans

It was not until the Enlightenment at the end of the 18th century that scientists began to classify the natural world in a systematic way. The German scholar George Agricola (1494–1555) made the first attempts to classify minerals and explain their origins, but it was not until the Scottish geologist James Hutton (1726–97) demonstrated that the earth was actually much older than anyone believed, that geology and its attendant disciplines really took off. Geological classification continued during the 19th century, but in earlier times, gems were categorized by their colour or place of origin. This meant that stones of a similar appearance were sometimes mistaken for one another and that some precious gems are not actually what they seem. A large red stone in the British Imperial State Crown, long believed to be the Black Prince's ruby, is actually a spinel, which is a bit like substituting a cubic zircona for a diamond. The French made a similar mistake, and Anne of Brittany's ruby, which adorns Louis XV's Order of the Golden Fleece, is also a spinel. Spinel is an attractive and costly gemstone in its own right. But it's not a ruby. A large stone in the Portuguese crown jewels, known as the Braganza diamond which was mined in Brazil in the 18th century, is more likely a very fine topaz or white sapphire.

o It was only in the late 18th century that the natural world began to be classified in a systematic way, which led to the renaming of some stones that had previously been mistaken for something else.

33

DIAMONDS

For centuries precious gems belonged solely to those at the top of the social and economic tree – royalty and the nobility. From the Egyptian pharaohs to the surviving crowned heads of Europe, kings and queens, princes and princesses, adorned themselves with the finest gems on offer. In most societies, the finest jewels were reserved to display a monarch's wealth, to dazzle both his friends and enemies with his power and opulence. They came to symbolise the unique power and position of rulers the world over. It was not until the more meritocratic 20th century that the actress Marilyn Monroe could sing about

diamonds being a girl's best friend – before that time, diamonds were rarely seen in the hands of commoners.

The British Crown jewels have a long and surprisingly chequered history, although they are still regarded as the most valuable set of jewels in history. Although the famous St Edward's Crown (the coronation crown) dates back to the reign of Edward the Confessor (1042-1066), King John famously lost a large portion of the jewels in the Wash while on the run from the barons in 1216, and during the 17th century Oliver Cromwell ordered them to be broken up. Although many of the gems survived to be reset, several of the Stuart and Hanoverian monarchs were forced to borrow jewels for their coronation regalia from London gem dealers. Fortunately, however, at the height of empire in the 19th century, the Crown received some of the finest diamonds in the world. Some, like the Koh-i-noor, were acquired in dubious circumstances of war and conquest, and others like the Cullinan were mined in the far-flung parts of the empire on which the sun never set.

The largest diamond ever mined was the Cullinan, found in South Africa in 1905 and weighing 3,106.75 carats (621.35g). Detectives from London were sent to South Africa to accompany the stone to England, but were actually a diversionary tactic – the diamond was put into a large box and shipped via parcel post. It was cut into four large jewels and presented to King Edward VII. Cullinan I also known as the Great Star of Africa was set into the monarch's sceptre; Cullinan II is set into the Imperial State Crown – usually worn by the Queen at the annual opening of parliament. Cullinan III and IV were installed in Queen Mary's crown.

The Koh-i-noor diamond, one of the largest single diamonds in the world was given to Queen Victoria in 1851. It was not only the most fabulous diamond then extant, but it also had a remarkable history – previous owners included Shah Jehan, the man who built the Taj Mahal, and Nadir Shah who captured it when he invaded Agra and Delhi in 1739. Nadir Shah knew that the defeated Indian prince had hidden it in his turban, and invited him to exchange turbans with him as a sign of brotherhood. When the stone rolled out, Nadir exclaimed 'Koh-i-noor', which means 'mountain of light', the name which has remained with the diamond ever since

The diamond, which has never been brought or sold and has only changed hands through conquest, has acquired a reputation as a bringer of bad luck: after his victory in Delhi, Nadir Shah suffered years of turbulent rule and was murdered in 1747. His empire broke up and the diamond fell into the hands of the Afghani rulers, who squandered three generations in internecine fighting, with the Koh-i-noor at the centre of it. Finally, it was surrendered to the British at the end of the Sikh wars and the Governor-General Lord Dalhousie, who firmly denied any rumours of curses or bad luck sent it to Queen Victoria. It was re-cut by Prince Albert and was most recently reset in 1937 in the consort's crown, worn by Queen Elizabeth the Queen Mother.

The story of the Koh-i-noor certainly captured the imagination of the Victorian public, many of whom who queued to see it at the Great Exhibition in 1851. The novelist Wilkie Collins used the legend in his great 1868 mystery novel The Moonstone, noting in his preface that it was one of the sacred gems of India and 'the subject of a prediction, which prophesied certain misfortune to the persons who should divert it from its ancient uses.'

The famous Hope Diamond was another magnificent gem which had been stolen from a holy Hindu sculpture in the 17th century, had passed through the hands of the French royal family and finally ended up with Hope family in England. The diamond was allegedly cursed by the Brahmin priests who noticed it had gone missing, and has since been blamed for the demise of the house of Bourbon and the tragedies which befell the Hope family in the late 19th and early 20th centuries. It is now on display in the Smithsonian Institute in Washington.

What these stories prove more than anything is that people believe in the mysterious powers attributed to crystals.

40

BIRTHSTONES

Most sources agree that the allocation of birthstones is random affair. It is a practice that was really only introduced in the late 18th century, although for centuries certain stones had been affiliated with particular months of the year and the whole idea probably had something to do with the 12 gemstones which were placed in the breastplate of the Jewish high priest. The whole practice can perhaps best be illustrated by the fact that gem stone associations and dealers can suggest additions to the list for each month of the year. In 2002, for example, the American Gem Trade Association announced that tanzanaite would join turquoise and zircon as the official birthstone for December. And why turquoise has any significance for December is anyone's guess – it isn't even a Christmassy colour!

In ancient India, gems were associated with the signs of the zodiac and the planets, and people believed that you good acquire good fortune by wearing a stone that was in harmony with the ruling planet.

When comparing the various lists of birthstones, it is important to remember that the older lists were compiled using stones which were readily available, whereas the list produced by gem traders today uses more 'glamorous' and expensive stones.

Traditional Birthstones

JANUARY	GARNET	
FEBRUARY	AMETHYST	
MARCH	JASPER or BLOODSTONE	
APRIL	SAPPHIRE	
MAY	CHALCEDONY, AGATE or EMERALD	
JUNE	EMERALD, AGATE or CHALCEDONY	

Traditional Birthstones

JULY	ONYX, CARNELIAN or SARDONYX	
AUGUST	CARNELIAN or SARDONYX	
SEPTEMBER	PERIDOT or SARDONYX	
OCTOBER	AQUAMARINE or BERYL	
NOVEMBER	TOPAZ	
DECEMBER	RUBY	

CRYSTALS FOR LIFE

In this section we shall examine how to choose the most suitable crystals for your needs, and how to take care of them so that they can be kept in optimum condition for use in crystal healing therapies. There are a variety of ways in which crystals can be used for healing. Don't forget that as well as directing their energies to people, they can also be used to cleanse or recharge your house or office. Some will even help your plants grow healthy! Crystal energy is all-embracing, so tune into it and use it wisely.

CHOOSING CRYSTALS

There are no hard and fast rules to abide by when it comes to choosing crystals. The stones you choose may be rough or polished, tumbled or cut, large or small, clear or coloured. In the first instance, selecting stones is a purely aesthetic experience – you may well find that that you are drawn to the most attractive stones at first. Linger a few moments, however, and let your instinct guide you to the stones that you need and will help you most. Always follow your intuition: if you trust your feelings you can be sure that the crystal you are drawn to is the right one for you at this particular time in your life. The well-meaning advice of friends or shop assistants is no doubt kindly meant, but only you can feel the connection with a particular crystal, so shut out the world for a few moments and listen to your feelings.

If you feel an immediate attraction to a crystal, trust your instinct and buy it. It's rather like meeting a stranger for the first time when you have an immediate gut reaction to them, whether it be a feeling of strong antipathy or instant attraction. You may not be able to explain your feelings in logical or rational terms, but you can simply sense inside whether or not you are on the same wavelength. Unlikely though it sounds, it's the same with stones. Humans and crystals share a number of mineral elements and both crystals and humans have their own frequencies. If one stands out, it may be because you are on the same frequency – this is the crystal for you! The crystals that appeal most to you are likely to be those that vibrate on a similar frequency to you.

48

People find their crystals in different ways and it should always be a magical and joyous experience. One of the most surprising places for me was a museum shop, where there was a fine collection of rough and tumbled crystals – I really shouldn't have been that surprised: it was a geological museum after all! Many people find crystals themselves in mountains, forests or on their travels; other receive them as gifts and theses days you can buy them all over the place, even over the internet.

Remember that life is a journey and that change affects us all, so the crystals that are right for you today may not always be the most effective ones for your needs. There will come a time when either you or your crystal will move on. If you have an overwhelming urge to give one of your crystals to a friend, just do it. Follow your instinct in the knowledge that the crystal has fulfilled its purpose with you and could be more valuable and useful to someone else. Let it go willingly and with love, and no doubt a new crystal will shortly 'find' you. It is easy to become attached to particular stones, but this may be a mistake as it is easy to lose stones and it is a very common experience. (Perhaps the exception to this is in the case of jewellery that may be prized for reasons of both sentimental attachment and value.) If one of your crystals disappears, try not to be too distressed: it is an indication that the crystal has served its purpose and that it is time for both of you to move on.

If a crystal is attuned to your vibrations it will communicate with you. You may experience a variety of sensations when you see it for the first time:

- heat emanating from the crystal

- cold energy

- a sudden burst of energy similar to an electric charge

- tingling in your fingers

- a pulsing or vibration

- an inner knowledge

- a feeling of balance and wholeness

- a wave of heat emanating your body

- warmth in your heart

- an overwhelming sensation of love

- a perfume emanating from the crystal

- colours surrounding the crystal

- a flash of light from the crystal

- a moistness in your hands

- the crystal apparently 'jumping out' at you or literally falling at your feet

- a sudden rush of excitement

- a protective feeling

- an urge to laugh

- shivers down your spine

- a light-headed sensation

- a sound in your ears

- changes in your breathing

- the knowledge that you just have to have it!

HEALING CRYSTALS

Crystals are available to the collector in many different forms. You can purchase rough stones in their natural state, or polished stones that have been tumbled in large rotating drums filled with water. Fine sand is added at a later stage to polish them further, a process that takes several weeks. More valuable stones, such as opals, rubies or quartz, may have been cut by a jeweller to enhance their shape.

O Rough and smooth examples of red jasper

NATURAL FORMS

Geodes

A geode is produced when a group of minerals grow together in a small hole or cavity within a rock. Geodes vary enormously in size – some are the size of a house, while most are the size of a man's fist. Healers believe that their womb-like appearance enhances the protective qualities of the crystals within them.

O Chalcedony geode.

Clusters

Clusters are many-pointed crystals embedded or fixed on to a rock base. The crystals can be large or small, and they are often placed in rooms to change the energy of the environment or to cleanse the room and convert negative energies into positive energy. They are also useful to cleanse and activate other crystals and are recommended in the workplace for their ability to deflect the stress and tension of others away from you.

O Amethyst cluster.

Single-terminated crystal

A single-terminated crystal has one flat end and one pointed, or terminated end. The energy is focused at the terminated end and these crystals are used mainly for healing and meditation, with the healing powers concentrated through the point of the crystal.

○ Single-terminated crystal.

Double-terminated crystal

Double-terminated crystals have points at both ends, enabling energy to move in one or both directions and to be transmitted or drawn in at either end. These crystals may be placed under the pillow to encourage peaceful dreams, or carried to provide protection during the day. These crystals occur naturally, but can also be manufactured

Barnacle crystal

A barnacle crystal is one that is covered, or partly covered, with smaller crystals. They are sometimes called teaching crystals, the large crystal being the teacher, or 'old soul' and the smaller ones the pupils who have been attracted to the wisdom of the larger stone.

Bridge crystal

A channelling crystal has a seven-sided face on the front of the crystal's terminated end, and a triangular face on the opposite side (back) of the terminated end. Such as crystal may be employed for channelling information, truth and wisdom form the spiritual realms.

Elestial or el crystal

The elestial crystal is recognised by its natural terminations and the growth of smaller crystals over the body and face of an etched or multi–layer crystal. It can sometimes look as though one crystal has grown over another, or as though candle wax has dripped onto it.

Elestials activate the third eye, remove negative energy blocks, balance the male and femal energies and assist with meditation. It is said that they carry the memory of all that existed in the world prior to the arrival of humanity.

O Elestial crystal.

Manifestation crystal

A small crystal that is totally enclosed by a larger one is called a manifestation crystal. They are quite rare and may be used for manifesting the highest good.

Phantom crystal

A phantom crystal can be recognised by its 'phantom' – an image of the structure of another crystal visible within the crystal. The phantom outline may be either partial or complete. These crystals are useful for spiritual development.

Record-keeper crystal

A record-keeper may be recognised by one or more raised triangles or pyramid shapes on one or two faces. Ancient wisdom and secrets are said to be stored within these crystals and are excellent for use in meditation.

Twin crystal

Two crystals that have grown together are known as twin crystals. These are especially useful in healing when two people are working on a relationship or working together. Also known as a 'soul mate crystal', it can help to draw a soul mate into your life.

O Twin crystal.

O Slice of blue agate.

Slices

Sometimes a stone is cut to reveal its inner beauty. Crystal slices are ideal for meditation and may also be placed in a room or on the body for healing purposes.

57

Doughnuts

A doughnut is, as its name suggests, a stone with a hole in it. Naturally occurring doughnuts are rare, but they are often carved in India and Nepal. They are ideal for meditation and for gazing into other dimensions. They may also be used to draw energy toward you and to clear a blocked chakra. Stones with naturally formed holes are regarded as symbols of good luck.

○ Amethyst doughnut

Eggs

Crystals may be fashioned into egg shapes by dealers. Apart from being very decorative, they fit perfectly into the hand and are ideal for meditation. Opaque stones such as jade, chalcedony and rhodonite look wonderful with their variegated lines of colour, but clear quartz is also beautiful. Such smooth stones are useful as acupressure or massage aids, or they can be used as 'worry beads' and handled to relieve stress and tension.

Crystal balls

Crystal balls or spheres may either be natural or man-made – highly polished balls are usually shaped from a larger piece of crystal. They usually have planes or flaws within them, and these are highly valued by those who indulge in scrying. Healers believe that they emit energy equally in every direction.

Pyramids

Pyramid–shaped crystals focus and amplify their energy through their apex. They are often used to change and preserve objects.

METHODS OF CHOOSING CRYSTALS

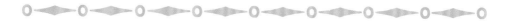

The following suggestions for choosing crystals are most useful when selecting a stone from your collection to use in a healing session – it is not always practical to use these methods in a small crystal shop!

Choosing with your eyes

a. Spread out the crystals in front of you. Close your eyes and take a few deep breaths to clear your mind.

b. Quickly open your eyes and pick up the first crystal that catches your eye.

It may not be the biggest, most beautiful or most expensive stone, but the fact that you were drawn to it suggests that it is attuned to your needs.

Scanning

Begin by shaking your hands to release any blocked energy. Briskly rub the palms of your hands together to concentrate energy in them and increase your sensitivity.

a. Close your eyes and take a few deep breaths to clear any negativity from your mind and body.

b. Very slowly run your hand over all of the stones without opening your eyes. If you are right-handed use your left hand, and vice-versa. Do you feel any of the sensations described earlier, such as heat, cold or tingling? At least one crystal should draw you to it like a magnet. Another common perception is that one stone feels sticky – if so, this is the stone you should select.

Vibration

a. Lay out the crystals in front of you and shake out your hands to release any blocked energy.

b. Vigorously rub the palms of your hands together to sensitise them. Take a few deep breaths to calm your mind and increase your focus.

c. Pick up each crystal in turn, sensing any vibrations. If you are left-handed, use your right hand, and vice-versa.

d. If the vibration of any of the stones resonates with you, then that is the correct crystal for you.

Using a pendulum

Using a pendulum is easy and it is an excellent way to enhance your intuition. A pendulum can be a crystal suspended on a chain or thong, although some are made of wood or metal. You can even use a key or ring, but if you do use an everyday object, make sure it is something personal. Using a pendulum to select a crystal is a little like dowsing and becomes easier the more you practise.

O A selection of pendulums suitable for dowsing.

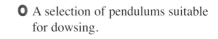

O A handmade pendulum will enable you to choose the crystal that is meant for you.

Holding a pendulum correctly.

Holding a pendulum incorrectly.

a. Gently hold the pendulum's string or chain between your thumb and index finger with the excess chain in the cup of your hand. Do not grasp it too tightly, and make sure that your neck and shoulders are relaxed.

b. Either mentally or out loud, ask the pendulum which movement indicates a yes answer. The pendulum will usually swing in a circular motion to indicate affirmative answers. To check its accuracy ask a couple of questions to which the answer is definitely yes, for example, 'My name is….Is that correct?'

c. When the pendulum has stopped moving, ask it which way it will move to indicate a negative answer. Take note of which way it moves.

d. Do the same thing for a 'don't know' answer. The pendulum will probably swing from side to side or move up and down to indicate uncertainty.

e. Once you are certain of the pendulum's movements, hold it over each crystal in turn and ask it 'Is this crystal right for me?', or 'Is this crystal suitable for healing/meditation?'

f. If you are dowsing over a large number of stones, pass the pendulum very slowly over the top of them to see whether the pendulum starts to react above any particular stone. Return to any 'reactive' stones and ask the question while positioning the pendulum directly above them.

You can also use this procedure to choose a crystal for a friend.

65

CARING FOR YOUR CRYSTALS

Crystals should be treated with care and respect. Some are harder than others, so be careful when storing them, as some are easily chipped or scratched (See page 132 for an explanation of crystalline hardness). It is worth wrapping them individually to transport them. Tumbled stones are probably the hardest, whereas crystal clusters are the most fragile. Remember that if you carry a crystal in your bag, it might chip or scratch possessions such as mobile phones, and note the danger posed to the crystal by keys or coins.

If you wear crystal jewellery such as a necklace, a bracelet or earrings, remove them when washing or swimming to avoid damage or loss.

O Tumbled stones are the most suitable for carrying in your pocket since they are fairly hardy.

O Crystal clusters are less durable

67

Cleansing crystals

It is vital to cleanse your crystals because they absorb all sorts of energies, both positive and negative. Cleansing is not simply about removing dust and grime – it is more about restoring positive energies to your crystals. It is especially important to cleanse new acquisitions, because they have passed through many hands before reaching you, and will have accumulated the energies and imprints of those who mined and transported them. Millions of years old, your crystals will have been examined by many prospective purchasers, so it is possible that they have accumulated negative thoughts which could be passed on to you. Don't forget to cleanse the crystals around your home from time to time. The negative energies that they absorb must be purged periodically so that the crystal can operate as effectively as possible.

There are several methods of cleansing crystals, but never use detergents or even soap – they can have an adverse effect in both physical and vibrational terms.

○ Cleansing with natural water.

1. Water cleansing

The easiest method is simply to hold your crystal under flowing cold water for several minutes. If you can take it to the sea, a spring or a clear flowing stream, so much the better, as the crystal will be revived by the natural energies of nature. If this is not possible, hold your crystal under running tap water for several minutes and imagine all the negative energies being washed away and dissolved. Alternatively, you could pour bottled spring water over it. Never wipe dry your crystals with a cloth or towel; instead leave them to dry naturally, preferably in the sun, which will re-energise them. Those born under the water signs of the western zodiac (Cancer, Scorpio and Pisces) will find water cleansing especially effective.

Cleansing with salt water

Salt and salt water are extremely effective cleansers, but some crystals should not be cleansed in this way because of a potential chemical reaction that may damage them. Delicate crystals include opal, carnelian, calcite, haematite, mica, turquoise and lodestone.

O Cleansing with salt water.

There are two ways of using salt to clean robust crystals. You can add a handful of sea salt to a bowl of warm water and immerse your crystals for a few hours. When you remove them, rinse the crystals thoroughly in running water and allow them to dry naturally. When you tip away the salt solution, be careful not to touch it, as you may absorb some of the negative energies within it.

You can also use dry salt to cleanse crystals. Simply pour out a quantity of sea salt into a bowl and bury your crystal in it. Leave for 24 house, then rinse thoroughly. This is not recommended for crystal clusters, because the salt may get stuck in the crevices of the rock and damage or split it.

A safer method is to place your crystal in a small glass dish, and then place the dish in a larger bowl full of salt. Even though the stone is not in direct contact with the salt, the cleansing process will still be effective. In both cases, discard the salt after use.

O Alternative salt-cleansing method.

Cleansing with holy water

You can also rub a few drops of holy water on your crystals to purify them and lift their vibrations. There are many sacred sites around the world where you can collect holy water, such as Glastonbury, the River Jordan or Lourdes.

O Cleansing with holy water.

2. Earth cleansing

Earth cleansing is particularly suited to those born under an earth sign in the western zodiac (Capricorn, Taurus and Virgo). Bury your crystal in your garden and leave it for at least 24 hours – and make sure you remember where you buried it! It is sensible to mark the spot, but make sure that any pets cannot dig it up. Alternatively, if you do not have a garden, or if the soil is acidic (which could damage the stone) bury your crystal in a plant pot. If you feel that your crystal has an especially strong charge that must be dispersed, leave it in the ground for up to a week. When you remove your stone from the earth, rinse it thoroughly in pure water and let it dry naturally.

3. Sun and moon cleansing

Simply leave your crystals outside for 24 hours (preferably when the moon is full) so that they can absorb the vigour of the sun's rays and the energy from the full moon. If you cannot leave them outside, place them on a sunny windowsill. Please be aware that long exposure to sunlight may cause delicate crystals such as amethyst, celeste, opal and turquoise to fade, and it is probably better to use moon cleansing for those stones.

4. Fire cleansing

Those born under the fire signs of the zodiac (Aries, Leo and Sagittarius) will find fire cleansing particularly helpful.

Light five or six tea lights and arrange them in a circle around your crystal. Leave them until they burn out.

Another method is to light a candle and very quickly pass your crystal through the flame (this method is not suitable for opals because they can be damaged by fire).

○ WARNING: Never leave burning candles unattended.

5. Smudging

Smudging is a traditional method of cleaning rooms and auras as well as crystals. Those born under air signs (Gemini, Libra, and Aquarius) will find this method effective. Smudging plays an important role in Native American traditions, when tightly rolled bunches

of herbs or plants were used to purify sacred objects. You can either make your own smudge stick or buy one from a New Age shop, or use an incense stick. Sage, cedar, lavender and sweet grass are common purification agents.

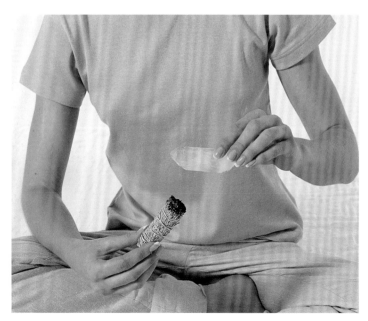

Light the smudge stick bundle at one end and as it catches fire, blow it out so that it is just smouldering. Slowly move your crystal through the smoke so that every facet is touched by it and negative energy removed by the air.

If you prefer you could use a feather or your hand to waft the smoke towards your crystal. Make sure you have a small bowl or ashtray to catch any ash and to stub out the smudge stick safely.

6. Cleansing with a crystal cluster

Place your crystal on a large quartz crystal cluster or a bed of amethyst. Leave it there for a few hours to neutralise any negative vibrations. This is especially good for polished or tumbled stones, which can benefit from the power emitted by crystals in their natural state.

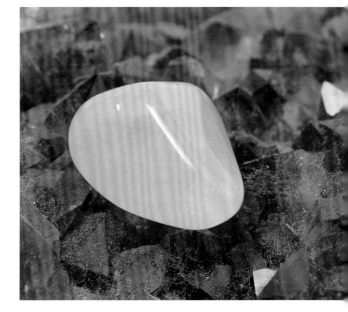

7. Flower cleansing

A beautiful and gentle method of cleansing is to bury your crystal in some flower petals. Pink rose petals are ideal for cleansing rose quartz, while lavender is useful for purifying purple stones such as amethyst. Collect some petals and flowers from your favourite plants and place them in a glass container. Bury your crystal underneath them and leave it there for 24 hours.

8. Rice cleansing

To cleanse your crystal using rice, fill a glass bowl with organic, uncooked brown rice and bury the crystal in the rice. Wait for twenty-four hours before removing it, by which time the rice will have absorbed any negative vibrations. The rice rice should be discarded after use and should not be eaten.

9. Mantra cleansing

A simple mantra such as 'Om' may be employed to cleanse your crystals. 'Om namah Shivaya' calls upon the Hindu god Shiva, the destroyer or transformer and is highly effective in clearing negative energies. Repeat your favourite mantra over your crystal and visualise the negative energies being replaced by pure ones.

Alternatively you could just pray over your crystal and ask the divine power to cleanse it thoroughly.

10. Essential oil cleansing

Aromatherapists are keen on this method of cleansing crystals. Useful essential oils are lavender, sage, cedarwood, lemongrass, pine, juniper, rosemary, lemon rosewood or vetivert.

Shake a couple of drops of essential oil onto a cloth and wipe it over your crystal to purify it.

Another method is to use an essential oil burner. Put a few teaspoons of water into the bowl on top of the diffuser. Light the tea light underneath and sprinkle a few drops of oil into the water. As the vapour begins to rise, hold your crystal in it and waft the steam around it.

Crystals appear to enhance the aroma of an essential oil. One drop of essential oil placed on a crystal is very powerful and can easily perfume an entire room; the aroma also seems to last for longer.

77

Dedicating your crystals

Once your crystals are cleansed and recharged, it is
important to dedicate them, as this ensures that they will
only be used in a positive way for the higher good of all.
It also protects the crystal from anyone who may try to
abuse its power. Crystalline energy can be channelled for
negative purposes as well as positive ones.

Hold your crystal in your hands and imagine
that it is surrounded by protective light. Say,
'I dedicate this stone to be used for the
universal good of all'.

Programming crystals

Crystals can be programmed for a multitude of purposes, including healing, meditation
and grounding. Quartz crystals are the most suitable for programming because they are
colourless – coloured crystals already have a programme of uses governed by their
colour and mineral compositions. Before you begin to programme a crystal, you
should be very clear about your intent. Crystals can
be programmed for the many purposes, among
them:

- self-healing
- healing others
- absent healing
- meditation
- angelic contact
- protection
- harmony
- love
- peace of mind

○ Quartz crystals are best for programming
  as they are colourless.

78

- interpretation of dreams
- scrying (crystal gazing)
- manifestation
- improving your environment

- vitality and energy
- stress relief
- past-life recall
- grounding

Once you have decided on your intent, hold your crystal in front of your heart chakra (the centre of your chest) and take a few deep breaths to focus your consciousness and feel the connection with the crystal.

Lift the crystal so that it is level with your third eye chakra (middle of the forehead) and state your intention clearly. You can either say it out loud, or repeat it inside your head: 'I programme this crytal to be used for healing, meditation, manifestation and communication with the angelic realms'. Repeat your intention several times to make your purpose clear.

You will intuitively know when the programming is complete. When it is, take a couple of deep breaths to detach your consciousness from the programmed crystal and put it down.

HOW TO USE
YOUR CRYSTALS

Crystals can be used in many ways – they can improve your well-being; bring harmony to your surroundings simply as decorations or to provide energy; they can be used to aid meditation or for healing

One of the easiest ways to tap into crystal energy is simply to wear one as a piece of jewellery. In this way the healing or protective power of the crystal is with you all day. It is best to wear one next to the skin, perhaps as a pendant or earrings. The crystal should be worn until there is a positive improvement in health, but don't be alarmed if initially, symptoms worsen. This is a good sign and shows that the body's self-healing mechanism has been revived. However, if this decline does not halt within a few hours, remove the crystal and wear it three times a day for about half an hour each time.

Crystals can also be carried in a pocket, but make sure you place them in a pouch to prevent it from becoming scratched or chipped. Hold the crystal when you feel in need of its support and absorb its healing energies directly through your skin. A set of worry beads made from your favourite stones is an excellent stress reliever.

Crystals can be used to improve your workspace – they can be used as book ends, paper weights, or simply placed in a bowl on your desk. Their natural beauty will cheer up the office, and their healing powers will protect you from the harmful effects of electromagnetic fields. Think about how your workplace could be improved and choose the crystals accordingly. Clear quartz is one of the best for dispersing electromagnetic fields, but must be cleansed regularly. If you need to improve your focus, place a piece of black obsidian on you desk; if you find you need to calm down, use a green stone such as peridot or jade to reduce stress. Moonstone is popular because it disperses tension and improves communication – vital to the smooth running of any office.

You can also use crystals to decorate your home, placing transparent stones in front of a lamp to create a dramatic lightbox, for example. Change the crystal when you want to create a different effect, so use yellow for relaxation, red for energy, or blue for communication. You can use different crystals in each room to harmonise the energies of the space. So a dining room would benefit from carnelian and amber to stimulate appetite and guard against food fads; quartz is useful in a study to help creativity; soothing, restful stones such as rose quartz or amethyst will assist in ensuring a peaceful night's sleep, while aquamarine and turquoise will banish tension and ensure friendly interaction in the living room.

○ Light display.

Meditating with crystals

Meditation is used by many people all over the world to calm the mind and achieve inner peace – or simply to provide a break from a frenetic routine. Using crystals in meditation will greatly enhance your practice and enable you to reach higher spiritual levels. It is also useful to have an object on which to focus when you are learning to meditate, and a specially chosen crystal is perfect. Of course, the crystals will enhance the meditative state, allowing you to reach deep within yourself to gain new insights or solutions to troubling problems.

Members of the quartz family are the most popular crystals for meditative purposes, especially clear quartz, amethyst, rose quartz and smoky quartz. However, it is important that you choose whichever crystal feels right, so pick the crystal that resonates with you.

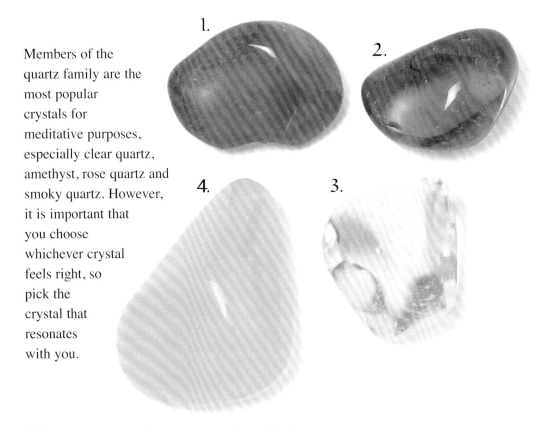

◦ Quartz crystals are the most popular for meditation.
1) Amethyst 2) Smoky quartz3) Clear quartz 4) Rose quartz

Meditation for beginners

It is unlikely that you will slip instantly into a meditative state the first time you try meditation – learning to still the mind and block out extraneous thoughts takes a little practice. But be patient and persevere as the rewards are well worth it.

How to meditate

1. Choose a time when you will not be disturbed. Unplug the telephone and tell everyone that you do not want to be interrupted.

2. Wear comfortable loose-fitting clothes and surround yourself with cushions for comfort.

3. Wrap a blanket around your shoulders in case you become cold while meditating.

4. Sit comfortably on the floor or on a chair. The ideal position is cross-legged on some cushions, but if this is uncomfortable, sit upright on a chair with your feet on the floor. It is important to hold your spine straight to establish a strong connection with the earth and enable your energies to flow freely.

5. Either hold your crystal gently, or place it in front of you and sit with your hands resting gently in your lap.

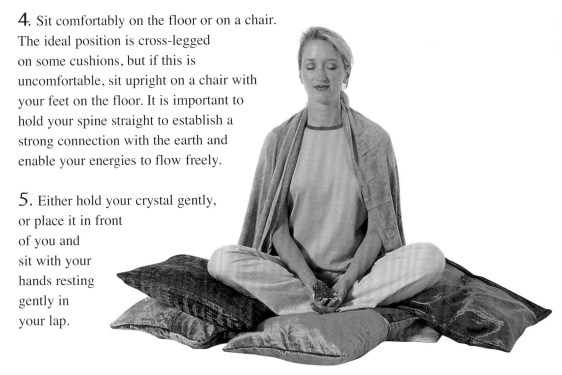

6. Focus your attention on the crystal. Notice its beauty, shape, form, and colour. If you are holding it, be aware of its weight and feel yourself absorbing its warmth and energies.

7. Close you eyes and become aware of your breathing. Take a few deep breaths from your abdomen. Inhale for a count of four, hold the breath for a count of two and exhale for a count of four. Continue breathing in this way until your mind is free of turbulence. Gently release any thoughts that pop into your head.

8. As you inhale feel your body take in the wonderful healing energies of your crystal, and as you exhale feel your tensions dissolve.

9. Allow yourself to sink gradually deeper into a meditative state. Feel your energy field expanding and filling with amazing crystalline energies.

10. Imagine that you are becoming part of your crystal. Allow your energy field to merge with that of the crystal so that you become one with it.

11. Allow yourself to enter the crystal and explore its magical inner kingdom. Or ask it a question. The first impression or thought that occurs to you will be the correct answer.

12. Remain in this blissful state for as long as you wish. When you are ready to return, become aware of your body and your contact with the earth. Gently move your fingers and toes and notice your surroundings.

13. Open your eyes. If you find it difficult to ground yourself, earth your energies by holding a piece of smoky quartz, black tourmaline or a Boji stone.

14. Write down your experience immediately as spontaneously as you can. Never dismiss any impressions or guidance that you felt as being unimportant.

Grounding

At the end of a meditation it is vital that you ground, centre and earth yourself. Some people find this much easier than others.

If you feel slightly detached from reality, 'spacey', dreamy or fuzzy-headed, hold a grounding stone such as black tourmaline, obsidian, haematite or smoky quartz in your hands until you feel more mentally stable. If you still feel a little light-headed, sip a glass of water. To earth yourself totally, go outside and stamp on the ground or go for a brisk walk. If you really need to be brought back down to earth, do a few mundane chores around the house or garden.

Crystal mandala meditation

A mandala is an ancient Buddhist and Hindu circular symbol that represents the universe. It is a wonderful aid to meditation as it helps to calm the mind and assists in self-healing. If you find it difficult to meditate, the very act of making a crystal mandala by laying out stones in a pattern will focus your mind and enable you to absorb the energies of the crystals. Gather your stones together (tumbled stones, crystal clusters and long or short crystals are all acceptable). Although you do not need to use them all, make sure that they have all been cleansed.

Sit on the floor and start to arrange the stones (if you would prefer to meditate from a chair, it is probably best to arrange the stones on a table). Place a piece of material on the floor or table to put them on. Silk, satin or velvet are all wonderful, but it really can be anything at all. Choose a crystal with which you have a particular affinity as your centrepiece.

There are no precise rules about the arrangement of stones in a mandala, so just follow your intuition and arrange them in a way that is pleasing to the eye.

Once your mandala is complete, try the following meditation either on your own, or with a partner or a group of friends.

a. Sit comfortably on the floor, with your back held straight. If you would prefer to sit in a chair, make sure it is upright and that your feet are flat on the ground to ensure a strong connection with the earth. Your crystal mandala should be in front of you.

b. Gently focus your eyes on the mandala. Observe the beauty of the patterns you have created and notice the colours and shapes of the crystals you have used.

c. Try placing your hands very gently on top of the stones to absorb their healing energies more completely.

d. Close your eyes and feel the warmth and energies emanating from the crystals. Allow yourself to slip into a meditative state. Remain in this peaceful reverie for as long as you wish.

e. When you are ready to return, open your eyes and notice how relaxed and tranquil you feel. Make sure that you feel earthed and grounded

Stone circle meditation

You don't need to travel to Stonehenge or any other ancient megalithic site to absorb the benefits of a stone circle meditation! This meditation involves arranging stones or crystals in a circle and then meditating within it. You will undergo physical, mental, emotional and spiritual changes as a result, and emerge revitalised and enriched by the experience.

There is no perfect size for a stone circle – you should simply feel comfortable with it. If you feel hemmed in or restricted, you should make it bigger. Conversely, if you are unable to feel the energy emanating from your crystals, you probably need to make it smaller. Nor are there any rules concerning the number of crystals you should use or what type. Be guided by your intuition.

If you are lucky enough to have a room in which you can leave your stone circle, you can spend a few minutes in it whenever you feel you need some peace and regeneration. This meditation is also wonderful outside in a quiet spot on a warm sunny day.

a. Gather together some cleansed crystals. Choose the crystal you would like to hold during the meditation.

b. Be guided by your intuition as you position the crystals around you.

Some people use only four healing crystals, arranging them on the compass meridians. Others use more – select as many as you wish.

c. Once you have arranged your crystals around you, settle yourself comfortably. If possible sit cross-legged in the middle of the circle, but if this is uncomfortable use an upright chair and plant your feet firmly on the ground.

d. Gently hold your chosen stone in your hands and take a few deep breaths in the spirit of love and peace to help disperse any stress or tension.

e. Close your eyes and feel yourself being totally enclosed by the healing energies of the crystals. Delight in the unconditional love, wisdom, peace and protection that they are bestowing on you.

f. Remain in your circle until you feel that you have absorbed the crystal energy. A few minutes may suffice, but equally, you may need 20 to 30 minutes to fully experience this.

g. When you feel ready to leave your stone circle, make sure that you are fully grounded.

Natural world meditation

If you enjoy meditating outdoors, try this exercise, which will make you feel very connected with the natural world around you. Although you can use any stone you wish, amber is an excellent choice, as it is an organic gemstone formed from the fossilised remains of pine tree resin, and has long been regarded as powerful healing stone.

a. Take a piece of amber and if possible find a pine tree – if there are none nearby, let your intuition guide you to another suitable tree.

b. Lean against the trunk of the tree while holding the amber in your hands.

c. Close your eyes and breathe deeply, absorbing the aromas of the tree and feeling the upright strength of the trunk against your spine. Imagine that you are drawing strength from the earth through your legs, hips and into the amber in your hands. Feel the energy flow through you into your back, shoulders, up into your head and into the tree trunk.

d. Relax and enjoy the feeling of being part of the natural universe.

e. When you are ready to end the meditation, open your eyes and stretch your arms wide. You should feel revitalised and wide awake, full of energy to tackle anything!

Cleansing quartz meditation

If you can set aside 15 minutes a day for meditation you will probably find that you feel refreshed and more able to cope with the vicissitudes of life. Use a quartz crystal to cleanse your mind and to re-energise you.

a. Either sit on the floor or in a chair with both feet on the floor. Hold a clear quartz crystal in your hands, and concentrate on it for a few minutes.

b. Shut you eyes and take several deep breaths to release any tension in your body.

c. Imagine that a shaft of white light is beaming down on your head and entering your body through the crown chakra. Try to feel the warmth of the light flowing down your spine into the core of your body, down your legs and through your feet into the earth. Relax and enjoy this feeling of tranquillity.

d. Finish by breathing deeply and flexing your hands and feet to ground yourself.

Crystal wands

Wands are the stuff of myth, legend and Harry Potter, but crystal wands are powerful healing tools that have been used for centuries by physicians, magicians and shamans. Their pointed shape means that their energies are focused and concentrated through the t ip. Some crystals naturally form wand shapes, but others have been artificially shaped and polished using the crystalline structure of the stone. It is possible to buy wands cut from virtually any crystal, such as amethyst, quartz, obsidian and fluorite, and it is worth consulting the A–Z section (page 130) where you will find information about the individual properties of each stone, before purchasing a wand. Some wands are formed from wood or metal and hold a crystal at their tip, while others have a quartz crystal at both ends. Whatever style you choose, use it judiciously and never point it at anyone unless you are healing them.

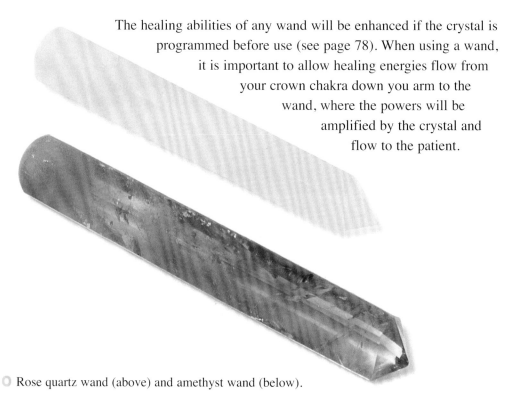

The healing abilities of any wand will be enhanced if the crystal is programmed before use (see page 78). When using a wand, it is important to allow healing energies flow from your crown chakra down you arm to the wand, where the powers will be amplified by the crystal and flow to the patient.

○ Rose quartz wand (above) and amethyst wand (below).

Using a crystal wand on a partner

Before you begin the healing session, make sure you will not be disturbed, dim the lights or light a few candles and prepare a well padded surface for your partner to lie on. Make sure that your partner has loose-fitting clothing and has removed any metal objects (such as coins or keys) from their person, as they produce false energy fields. Although this kind of healing session is probably more relaxing if the patient is lying down, it can be conducted sitting in a chair with both feet on the floor.

a. Cleanse and programme your wand in the same way as you would a crystal to make it ready for use. Make sure you have a piece of smoky quartz or similar grounding stone to hand for use at the end of the session.

b. Ask your partner to lie on their back with a cushion under their head and another under their knees. Ask them to relax by breathing deeply.

c. Position yourself at their head and using a featherlight touch, place your hands on their shoulders or head. When you are ready, ask for healing energy to flow through you. Ask your partner to take some deep breaths to inhale love and peace and exhale stress and tension.

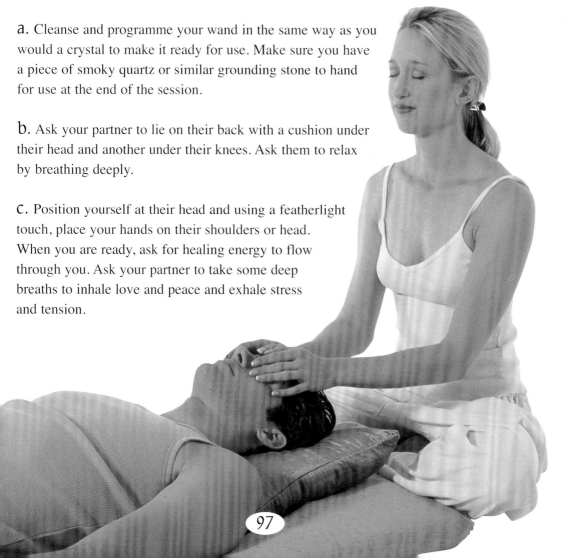

d. Stand up and pick up your wand
(which may feel as though it is
pulsating or tingling) and working in
a clockwise direction, gently move
the wand around the perimeter of the
body to cleanse their aura.

e. When you feel that you have removed any negative vibes, point your wand downwards toward the earth and ask the earth to transform the negative energy that it has absorbed into positive power.

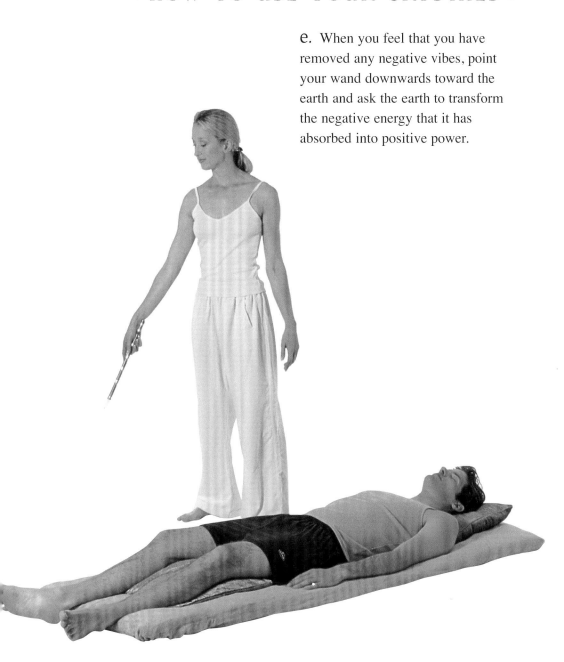

f. When you feel that the wand is recharged, point it at the areas of your partner's body that need healing. Work in a clockwise direction. Painful or diseased areas will be filled with healing light within a few minutes. Discharge the negative energy from your wand after you have treated each area, and then move on to the next one.

g. When you have finished, put your wand somewhere safe, ready to be cleansed. Pick up the piece of smoky quartz and place it at your partner's feet to stabilise and ground them. Gently rub their feet and lower legs to bring them back to full consciousness and ask them to open their eyes.

Scrying

Scrying is an ancient method of divining, either using crystals or a crystal ball to reveal the secrets of the past, present and future. The word comes from the Anglo-Saxon descry, which means to reveal. You can work with a large clear quartz crystal, a crystal ball or egg, or even a crystal pyramid. Once again, use your intuition when choosing a scrying crystal.

Although most are colourless, which appears to enhance communication, it is also possible to buy amethyst, selenite or obsidian crystal balls. Many crystals are sold via mail order, but it is important to hold a crystal ball before buying one, to make sure it feels right. Try to pick up several before you make your selection and choose the one with which you feel most comfortable.

When you have chosen your crystal ball cleanse it using one of the methods on pages 68 and leave it in view of the moonlight on the night of a full moon in order to charge it. Then wrap it safely in a cloth and don't let anyone else touch it.

Using a crystal ball

Crystal balls are not just for fortune-tellers at fairs – they can help you to evaluate a situation, whether it is a dilemma you face, or a friend's problem. Practitioners see a variety of things in crystal balls: some images are as clear as a film, while others are simply abstract symbols. It might be useful to consult a book of symbols or a dream dictionary after a scrying session, as they might throw some light on the symbols or images you have seen.

a. Spread out a cloth and put your crystal ball on it, resting it on its stand.

b. Dimming the lights and lighting a couple of candles might make it easier to read your crystal, but it is also perfectly acceptable to scry in daylight. Make yourself comfortable facing your crystal.

c. Focus on your breathing and take several deep breaths to release any stress and tension.

d. Hold your crystal ball for a while as you begin to focus on a question. Now put it down again.

e. Relax, cup your hands over the crystal ball and gaze into it. Do not focus on the surface, but try to look deep into it. It may appear to mist over with pictures or symbols, or else very definite images may enter your mind. If you don't gain an impression immediately, don't worry, and don't try to peer into your crystal to force a notion. You can always try again tomorrow and gazing into your ball little and often is more effective than staring at it for
prolonged periods.

f. Give thanks to you higher self and to the crystal for any insights you may have gained.

g. Write down any impressions that you received, even if they seem nonsensical. They might make sense later on.

h. Make sure you feel properly grounded – if necessary hold on to a grounding stone for a few minutes before wrapping up your crystal ball and putting it away.

CRYSTALS AND THE CHAKRAS

In ancient Indian philosophy, the chakras refer to seven main energy centre within the body. The word chakra comes from the Sanskrit for wheel, and healers and yogis believe that each chakra is like a vortex, a constantly revolving wheel of energy. The chakras are positioned in a line from the base of the spine to the top of the head, and each one is associated with a particular colour, an aspect of consciousness and has a specific function in keeping the physical, emotional and mental body in good health. It is important for the chakras to be balanced and to work in harmony, so that an individual can be happy and healthy. The chakras may be visualised as lotuses, each one possessing a different number of petals. New Age healers believe that the chakras spin to draw energy from the Universal Life Force. With their highly tuned vibrations, crystals embody some of the Universal Life Force and are therefore important in rebalancing the chakras and restoring health.

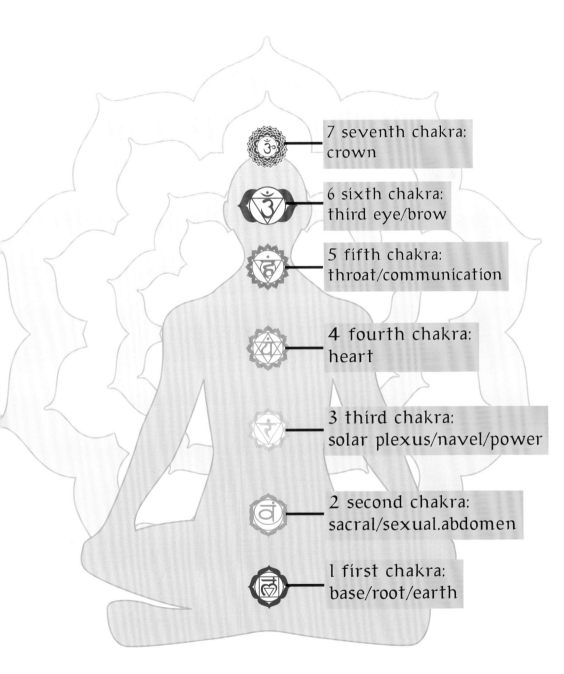

7 seventh chakra:
crown

6 sixth chakra:
third eye/brow

5 fifth chakra:
throat/communication

4 fourth chakra:
heart

3 third chakra:
solar plexus/navel/power

2 second chakra:
sacral/sexual.abdomen

l first chakra:
base/root/earth

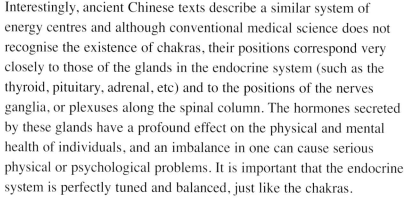

Interestingly, ancient Chinese texts describe a similar system of energy centres and although conventional medical science does not recognise the existence of chakras, their positions correspond very closely to those of the glands in the endocrine system (such as the thyroid, pituitary, adrenal, etc) and to the positions of the nerves ganglia, or plexuses along the spinal column. The hormones secreted by these glands have a profound effect on the physical and mental health of individuals, and an imbalance in one can cause serious physical or psychological problems. It is important that the endocrine system is perfectly tuned and balanced, just like the chakras.

Chakras act as bridges linking the physical body with the subtle bodies, also known as the aura or energy shield that surrounds all living things. Our chakras must be balanced to allow the free flow of energy or prana to ensure optimum health. If they are blocked, we suffer physical, mental or emotional unease.

THE SEVEN MAJOR CHAKRAS

First chakra - base chakra

Sanskrit name: Muladhara

Meaning: Root/support

Location: Base of the spine in the perineum between the anus and the genitals.

Colour: Red, signifying passion for life; or black, representing stability or grounding.

Petals: Four

Element: Earth

Associated glands: Adrenals; some believe gonads (i.e. testes or ovaries).

Function: The earth chakra is the centre of our survival and security and also relates to our potential. If it is imbalanced, our survival instincts are weakened, we are not grounded and do not have a strong physical will to be on earth. We will experience feelings of 'spaciness' and lack courage, stamina and strength. Physical signs of imbalance are manifested as problems with the feet, ankles and knees, lower back, and bowels. Sciatica or haemorrhoids are common if the bas chakra is blocked.

Chakra stones: Mostly red and black crystals – fire agate, bloodstone, Boji stone, red calcite, carnelian, cuprite, garnet, haematite, jasper (brown and red), obsidian, smoky quartz, ruby, black sapphire, black tourmaline.

Second chakra - sacral chakra

Sanskrit name: Svadhisthana

Meaning: Seat of vital force/sweetness.

Location: Lower abdomen a few inches below the navel.

Colour: Orange representing creativity and wisdom.

Petals: Six

Element: Water

Associated glands: Gonads (testes or ovaries); some say spleen.

Function: The sacral chakra is the sexual chakra, related to creativity and emotion. If it is unbalanced we experience problems forming relationships. An imbalanced sex drive, frigidity, impotence, loss of libido or conversely, promiscuity, are common problems. The reproductive organs may not function properly, leading to infertility. As this chakra is connected to the water element, there may be problems with the kidney, bladder or prostate gland.

Chakra stones: Orange stones such as carnelian, amber, orange calcite, citrine, golden labradorite, tangerine quartz, thulite and topaz.

Third chakra - solar plexus

Sanskrit name: Manipura

Meaning: Power chakra/ lustrous gem.

Location: Between the umbilicus and the solar plexus.

Colour: Yellow

Petals: Ten

Element: Fire

Associated glands: Pancreas (or adrenals)

Function: The solar plexus chakra is the source of our personal power and represents our analytical thought and intellectual activity. It is related to energy, assimilation and the metabolism. The solar plexus chakra enables us to transform our desires, emotions and ambitions into action, so an imbalance in this area leads to a lack of confidence and emotional instability. Other problems may be low self-esteem, addictions and an inability to relax. When it is healthy, it gives us energy, effectiveness and spontaneity. Physical signs of a problem include digestive troubles, diabetes, eating disorders, allergies and chronic fatigue.

Chakra stones: Yellow stones such as amber amblygonite, ametrine, golden beryl, citrine, yellow jasper, smoky quartz, yellow sapphire, sunstone, tiger's eye and yellow tourmaline.

Fourth chakra - heart chakra

Sanskrit name: Anahata

Meaning: Unstuck

Location: Centre of the chest.

Colour: Green (healing and balance) or pink (love and compassion).

Petals: Twelve

Element: Air

Associated glands: Thymus

Function: This, the middle chakra, is related to social acceptance and is the chakra of love and compassion. It also works to integrate opposites in the psyche – male and female, ego and unity, persona and shadow. Its colour is either green, which represents healing and balance, or pink which symbolises love. If this chakra is blocked, individuals are likely to be depressed, unable to love themselves and have difficulties forming relationships. Physical manifestations of trouble include circulatory disorders, blood pressure and heart problems, asthma or lung disease and a poor immune function.

Chakra stones: Green or pink stones, including amblygonite, green Aventurine, green calcite, charoite, chrysoprase, pink danburite, emerald, jade, green or pink fluorite, jasper, kunzite, malachite, morganite, peridot, green or rose quartz, watermelon tourmaline.

Fifth chakra - throat chakra

Sanskrit name: Visshuda

Meaning: Purification

Location: Throat

Colour: Blue

Petals: Sixteen

Element: Sound /ether

Associated glands: Thyroid

Function: The throat chakra is related to communication (both verbal and non-verbal), self-expression and creativity. A blockage in this chakra leads to an inability to express one's feelings and ideas. In physical terms, throat or hearing problems, neck and shoulder pain, and either stuttering or non-stop chatter signify that the throat chakra needs healing.

Chakra stones: Blue stones such as blue lace agate, amazonite, aquamarine, azeztulite, azurite, blue calcite, blue chalcedony, chrysocolla, blue fluorite, lapis lazuli, larimar, malachite, aqua aura quartz, blue sapphire, Shattuckite, blue tourmaline, turquoise.

Sixth chakra - third eye chakra

Sanskrit name: Ajna

Meaning: To command or know.

Location: Centre of forehead (representing the search for and attainment of spiritual purpose).

Colour: Indigo

Petals: Two

Element: Light

Associated glands: Pituitary (or pineal)

Function: The third eye or brow chakra enables us to see clearly, not only in physical terms, but perhaps more importantly, on an intuitive level. It enables us to reflect on 'the bigger picture', to gain a deeper understanding of our psychic abilities and to gain inner wisdom. Physical signs of an imbalance in this chakra include headaches, dizziness, eye disorders and nightmares. Psychological problems include hallucinations, living in a fantasy world and a lack of imagination and intuition.

Chakra stones: Mainly indigo, including amethyst, angelite, Azeztulite, azurite, blue calcite, charoite, purple fluorite, iolite, lapis lazuli, larimar, lepidolite, Shattuckite, tanzanite, turquoise.

Seventh chakra - crown chakra

Sanskrit name: Sahasrara

Meaning: To multiply by a thousandfold

Location: Top of head (anterior fontanelle of newbon babies)

Colour: White signifying purity, perfection or bliss, or violet, representing enlightenment.

Petals: One thousand

Element: Thought/knowing

Associated glands: Pineal or pituitary

Function: The crown chakra represents our connection to a world beyond our own, to the Universal Consciousness, a timeless place of all-knowing. It is our centre of spirituality and enlightenment and is related to self-knowledge. When well developed, individuals demonstrate wisdom, understanding, spirituality and bliss. Physical signs of problems are epilepsy, Alzheimer's disease, Parkinson's disease, memory disorders, obsessiveness and confusion.

Chakra stones: Mostly clear or violet stones, such as amethyst, ametrine, angelite, azeztulite, charoite, danburite, diamod, lepidolite, phenacite, clear quartz, selenite, sugilite and tanzanite.

115

CHAKRA HEALING

Each chakra of the body is associated with a particular colour, and colour affects everyone in different ways by reviving memories or old associations. The colour spectrum can also be used to represent the different energies at work in our bodies and specifically, our chakras. Of course, the most immediately striking aspect of any crystal is its colour and the interplay of light upon it. Hang a clear crystal in a sunny window and watch as the spectrum of colours dances on your walls – it is guaranteed to lift your spirits.

The ancient Egyptians based many of their remedies and healing potions on colour: red ingredients were used to treat blood disorders, and green ones for soothing headaches, for example. People wore clothes and jewellery in particular colours as a preventative measure to protect them against illnesses – red, for example, was meant to boost poor circulation and yellow was worn to cure impotence (and stupidity!) As late as the 19th century in Russia and Ireland, patients were wrapped in red flannel to treat scarlet fever and measles.

Using crystals in chakra healing is a reasonably simple matter of placing a suitable crystal on the chakra that needs work, and leaving it there for 15 minutes. Stones can be placed on any part of the body, or just above the head for the crown chakra and below the feet for grounding routines.

COLOUR HEALING CHART

CHAKRA	COLOUR	STONE	ACTION/EFFECT
Base/root/ earth	Red/black	Red jasper, haematite, carnelian, fire agate, bloodstone, black tourmaline, smoky quartz	Passion for life grounding (black stones)
Sacral/ sexual/ abdominal	Orange	Citrine, topaz, amber, thulite, carnelian, orange sunstone, tangerine quartz, orange calcite	Sensuality, creativity
Solar plexus	Yellow	Amblygonite, yellow jasper, amber, golden labradorite, tiger's eye	Release tension, increase confidence, alertness and happiness

Heart	Green/pink	Aventurine, green calcite, malachite, jade, amazonite, green jasper, emerald, kunzite, rose quartz, rhodochrosite	Promote unconditional love, compassion and healing, relationships
Throat	Blue	Angelite, blue lace agate, turquoise, aqua aura, chrysocolla, Shattuckite, aquamarine	Communication and expression
Third eye/brow	Indigo	Azurite, iolite, tanzanite, Azeztulite, sugilite, amethyst, charoite, blue calcite, lapis lazuli	Intuition, spiritual purpose, dreaming and sleep
Crown	Violet/clear	Charoite, angelite, clear quartz, Azeztulite, lepidolite, amethyst, danburite	Spirituality, imagination, connection to higher self

Balancing the chakras

If you would like to carry out a treatment for the whole body, you will need eight small stones, one for each chakra and a grounding stone for use at the end. Make sure they are all cleansed. You can carry this out alone, or treat a partner. Incidentally, you do not need to treat all the chakras at once. If you know which one needs work, simply place your chosen stone on the chakra that is out of alignment.

Solo treatment

a. Lie down on a padded surface in a peaceful room and make sure you will not be disturbed. Remove any metal items from your body.

b. Take several deep breaths to release any tension, then place each crystal on the appropriate chakra. Put the grounding stone near your feet.

c. Be aware of your breathing, which should be slow and steady.

d. Close your eyes and concentrate on each stone in turn. Feel the healing crystal energy revitalise each chakra in turn.

e. After about 15 minutes slowly open your eyes. Remove the stones one by one, beginning with the crown chakra. Stretch your feet so that they touch the grounding stone for a minute or two.

Balancing a partner's chakras

a. Ask your partner to lie down either on their front or back, whichever is most comfortable.

b. Place yourself at the receiver's feet. Take a few deep breaths to centre yourself and release any negativity. Ask you partner to do the same.

c. When you are both ready, gently place the seven stones on the chakra points of the receiver's body and leave them there for 15 to 20 minutes to allow the crystalline energies to become integrated into the chakras.

d. Remove the crystals very slowly one by one, beginning at the crown chakra and working downwards. Gently rub the receiver's feet and lower legs to balance and ground them.

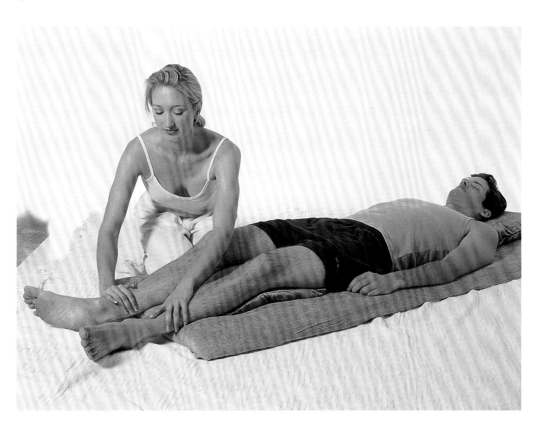

e. When the receiver is ready ask them to open their eyes. Give them a grounding stone to hold for a few minutes and offer them a glass of water.

123

Using a pendulum

Using a pendulum is not only an effective way to balance the chakras, but it is also an excellent method of assessing which areas need treatment before aligning them. (For tips on how to use a pendulum, see page xx)

The best crystals to use in pendulums are those with generalised energy, rather than those that have strong affinity for one particular chakra. Clear and transparent crystals are best, although quartz, amethyst and smoky quartz all make excellent pendulums as they will respond to and balance many different kinds of energy. Make sure you cleanse your pendulum regularly, especially before a healing session.

a. Ask you partner to lie on their back or front – whichever is most comfortable.

b. Hold the pendulum between your index finger and thumb, and suspend it just above the receiver's body over the base chakra. Do not be alarmed if it swings wildly – this is how it restores harmony to the energy centre.

c. Move up the body, holding the pendulum over each chakra in turn.

d. Once you have completed the treatment, ground the receiver by holding their feet, giving them an earthing stone to hold, and offering them a glass of water.

Crystal healing

Crystals can also be used to treat specific problems such as headaches, stress or swellings. When a body is in pain, it is tense, and crystal healing is effective because it calms and relaxes the patient. Remember that crystal healing should not be substituted for medical care as advocated by a qualified medical practitioner, although it can be an effective addition to a patient's care routine.

○ Crystals can be used to treat specific problems such as headaches or stress.

The following table provides a brief summary of where to place stones to relieve minor aches and pains. In each case, place or hold the crystal in position for several minutes and visualise the healing energy passing from the crystal to your body.

SYMPTOM	CRYSTAL	TREATMENT
Headache	Amethyst, violet stones with affinity to crown chakra	Lie down with one amethyst on the crown chakra and another on the third eye chakra.
Back ache	Clear quartz	Place crystal at crown chakra and imagine healing light passing down your spine with each breath.
	Lodestone	Place one piece at base of spine and another near the top of the neck to relieve back tension.
Tense muscles	Tourmaline (black or green)	Use tourmaline earrings to ease neck, jaw or head tension. In other parts of the body hold a piece of tourmaline near the affected area.
Inflammation	Malachite	Hold next to affected area

SYMPTOM	CRYSTAL	TREATMENT
PMS	Moonstone, opal	Wear moonstone jewellery to alleviate hormone-induced mood swings. Carry dark opal in your pocket to relieve menstrual pain.
Lack of energy	Garnet, amber, topaz, yellow citrine, clear quartz	Place a citrine stone on the solar plexus and hold a clear quartz point upwards in each hand.
Stress	Clear quartz, rose quartz tiger's eye	Place rose quartz over heart chakra, with four clear crystals pointing away from it. Put tiger's eye below the navel, surrounded by four clear crystals pointing towards it.
Sleeplessness	Chrysoprase	Place under pillow or beside bed.
	Tourmaline, smoky quartz, labradorite	Banish nightmares by placing next to bed.

A-Z OF CRYSTALS

In this section we have listed a wide range of crystals, noting their healing properties, as well as their geological origin and historical uses. It is not an exhaustive list, but it does cover those crystals that are relatively easy to obtain and are in common usage.

Classification

There are over 4,000 different types of mineral, with many more being discovered and classified each year. They are classified according to their chemical composition and internal molecular structure. Since 1941 mineral classification has been augmented by Hugo Strunz's system of using crystallography to examine chemical composition. Minerals are arranged into ten groups: Elements; Sulphides and Sulphosalts; Halides; Oxides; Carbonates; Borates; Sulphates; Phosphates; Arsenates and Vanadates; Silicates; and Organic compounds. Silicates comprise the largest group – almost a third of all minerals are silicates, which make up 90 % of the earth's crust, and of this group, quartz is the most common mineral on earth.

O Raw quartz crystal.

Geologists and mineralogists use a variety of criteria to identify the physical properties of rocks and minerals. They test hardness, density and how rocks break, for example, as well as subjecting them to tests to identify specific gravity and analysis of mineral content.

Hardness is measured on the Mohs scale, devised in 1812 by the German mineralogist Friederich Mohs. He took ten standard minerals ranging from talc (the softest) to diamond (the hardest). All minerals can be rated this way by assessing which they will scratch, and which will scratch them. This system can be replicated using fingernails, coins, iron nails, glass, pen knife, steel rasp sand paper and a knife sharpener.

The scale shows Moh's minerals with the everyday equivalents in brackets.

Moh's Scale:

1 Talc

2 Gypsum (fingernail)

3 Calcite (bronze coin)

4 Fuorite (iron nail)

5 Apatite (glass)

6 Orthoclas (pen knife)

7 Quartz (steel rasp)

8 Topaz (emery sandpaper)

9 Corundum (knife sharpener)

10 Diamond

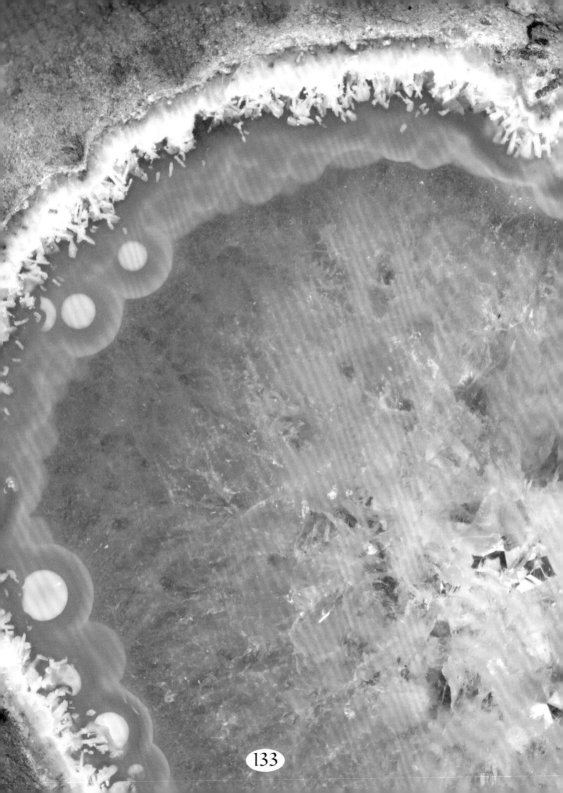

Colour and lustre

Most minerals and crystals are first identified by their colour, and in many crystals this is governed by the trace of impurities within them: these minerals are known as allochromatic and this classification covers virtually every coloured stone. Tiny traces of chromium and canadium turn beryl into emerald, for example, and impurities in clear quartz can turn it into almost any colour in the spectrum.

Lustre is the word used to describe the way the surface of the crystal appears – shiny, dull, metallic, etc. There are ten terms used to describe a crystal's lustre, most of which are self-explanatory:

Adamantine	– brilliant and shiny like a diamond and other gem crystals (from the Greek adamantos, meaning 'invincible')
Dull	– a non-reflective surface
Earthy	– a surface like dried mud
Greasy	– shiny, but slightly slimy in appearance
Metallic	– gleaming like metal
Pearly	– a milky shimmer just like a pearl
Resinous	– thick glow like sap or glue. (Most resinous minerals have a yellow/brown colour, like amber)
Silky	– a subtle shimmer
Vitreous	– shines like glass (eg quartz)
Waxy	– a dull waxy sheen

AGATE

Classification:	Silicate
Colour:	Several forms: blue, green, brown, yellow, banded
Hardness:	7
Lustre:	Vitreous or resinous
Rarity:	Common
Found:	Germany, Austria, Madagascar, Botswana, China, India, Australia, Brazil, Mexico, California, Arizona

Healing attributes: Stability, harmony, banishes negativity

Agate is a form of chalcedony, a quartz mineral that has formed at low temperatures in crystals so small that they seem more like porcelain. A translucent stone, agate occurs when traces of iron and manganese create bands in chalcedony and it is usually found in basalt cavities. It occurs in a variety of colours, including blue, white, grey, brown, red, green, yellow, black and rose. Some varieties occur only in one particular part of the world: brown Botswana agate, as its name suggests, is found only in Botswana, for example.

In India, Nepal and Tibet, agate amulets have been popular for centuries and were worn to bring protection and good fortune. In Biblical times, agate was one of the precious stones used in breastplate of the Jewish high priest, and healing powers were attributed to it in the medieval era, when it was regarded as a kind of universal antidote, rendering any poison useless. This stemmed from the popular belief that eagles placed agate stones in their nests to protect their young from venomous snakes. Red agate was believed to sharpen vision, and agate held in the hand or mouth was supposed to relieve a fever.

Agate is regarded as a very stable stone and is excellent for rebalancing and harmonising mind, body and spirit. It is also used to cleanse and stabilise the aura and to banish negative vibes. Agate helps to stimulate or strengthen analytical capabilities, encouraging clear thinking, rationality and enhancing concentration. In addition, agate helps us to gain access to, and inspiration from the spiritual world. Agate is traditionally used during pregnancy, because it helps to soothe, calm and centre both mother and baby during pregnancy and labour.

Specific types of agate also have other properties, which often relate to their colour.

Blue lace agate

Blue lace agate is usually pale blue with white or darker blue lines, lending it an ethereal, and soothing quality. It is especially effective if used on the throat chakra, encouraging freedom of expression, but it will also harmonise the heart, third eye and crown chakras. A calming stone, it emanates peace and tranquillity, enabling users to reach an elevated state of spiritual awareness. In physical terms, blue lace agate helps to accelerate and strengthen the repair of bones, as well as cooling arthritic inflammation. This cool stone soothes sore, red eyes, and any skin problem associated with redness and irritation.

Fire agate

A tumbled fire agate stone is almost an amber colour, although in its natural state it can incorporate swirling colours of brownish orange, blue and green. Fire agate is associated with the base chakra and is useful for grounding and establishing a powerful connection with the earth. This crystal empowers the owner, dispelling fear and providing a strong shield of protection to the wearer.

As its name implies, fire agate is linked to the fire element, so is extremely useful in symbolically 'burning away' old habits or facets of your life to make way for new, revitalised behaviours. It will help to destroy any blockages or obstacles that are impeding your progress. Fire is warming and energising, so fire agate can help to revive you when you are exhausted or 'burnt out'.

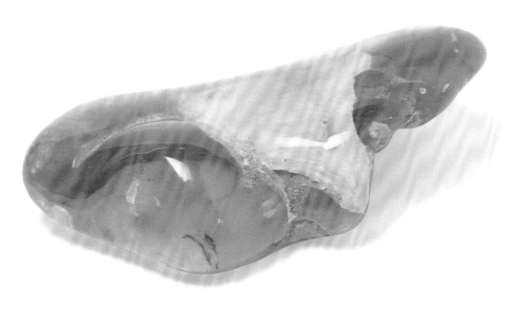

AMAZONITE

Classification:	Silicate
Colour:	Green
Hardness:	6-6.5
Lustre:	Vitreous
Rarity:	Common
Found:	USA, Russia, Canada, Brazil, India, Mozambique, Namibia, Austria
Healing attributes:	Empowering, boosts confidence, stabilises the metabolism

Amazonite, or amazon stone is a variety of the silicate microcline, an alkali feldspar, which forms tabular or short prismatic crystals. Despite its name, no deposits of amazonite have ever been found in the River Amazon. An opaque stone with a

beautiful green or turquoise colour (and a white streak), amazonite is occasionally mistaken for jade. Amazonite artefacts have been found among Ancient Egyptian relics, but it really became popular in the late 19th century when large deposits were discovered in Colorado.

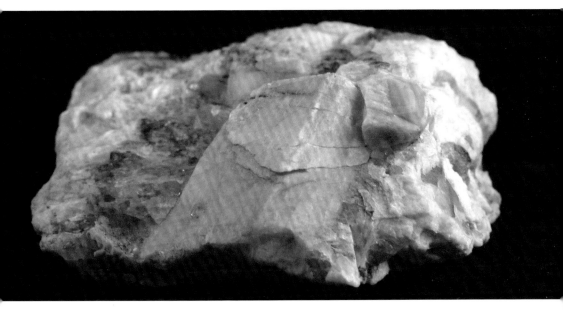

In healing, amazonite is gentle stone, particularly beneficial for the throat chakra, encouraging communication and supporting the thyroid and parathyroid. Many healers believe it endows courage and boosts confidence, perhaps because of the associations of its name with the formidable female Amazon warriors. It can help to balance the metabolism and regulate calcium deficiencies, while alleviating cramps and muscular spasms. Perhaps because of its soothing green colour, amazonite is wonderful for soothing and harmonising the nervous system, dispelling worries, fears, anger and irritation. It will help balance mood swings and restore your equilibrium. If you use amazonite you will feel encouraged to take charge of your life, feel empowered, and realise that you have the ability to change almost any situation.

AMBER

Classification:	Mineraloid (organic compound)
Colour:	Orange–golden brown, transparent
Hardness:	2+
Lustre:	Resinous
Rarity:	Commonly occurring
Found:	Britain, Canada, Dominican Republic, Italy, Germany, Lebanon, Poland, Romania, Mexico, Myanmar, Baltic Sea,
Healing attributes:	Purification of mind and body; good luck, mental stimulation

Amber is immediately identifiable by its smooth, rounded shape and lustrous orange-brown hue, but in geological terms, amber is not actually a crystal at all. It is a transparent or translucent fossilised pine tree resin, usually golden orange or brown in colour. It is a mineraloid, which means that it does not conform to the usual basic properties of minerals or fit easily into one of the classified chemical families. Amber is organic, that is, it originated with a living thing, and does not form crystals. It is a form of tree resin that hardened and was preserved over millions of years. It degrades when exposed to oxygen, so it is usually found in dense wet sediments such as clay and sand formed by ancient river beds or lagoons. It can be found washed up in shale on beaches, but there are large deposits in the Baltic and the Dominican Republic where it is mined.

The Greeks referred to it as elektron and in about 600 bc the philosopher Thales was the first to note amber's ability to attract bits of dust, seeds and hairs when rubbed. He was witnessing static electricity, and this is the source of the modern word electricity. Some six hundred years later, the Roman academic Pliny the Elder wrote in his Natural History that 'Amber is formed by the pith which flows from trees of the pine species, as a gum flows from cherry trees and resin from pines'. This was a remarkable piece of scientific understanding, which somehow disappeared from view for 1,500 years. Amber was a very popular decorative gem in Roman times, especially as a jewel. It was traded around the world and worked into beautiful jewellery by peoples from the Romans to the Celts, Anglo-Saxons, Chinese and Indians.

It has long been regarded as one of the most precious of all 'crystals', prized for its powerful healing properties over thousands of years, and often used as a remedy with a similar effect to penicillin. It has an affinity with the solar plexus and throat chakras and may also be used to treat the kidneys and bladder. A stone of purification, amber cleanses the mind, body and spirit, as well as the aura and one's environment. It draws disease out of the body, healing and renewing the nervous system and balancing the right and left sides of the brain. Amber also bestows joy and spontaneity, increasing confidence, and according to some, bringing good luck. Finally, in keeping with its fossilised origins, amber is regarded as possessing timeless wisdom and acts as a record-keeper of the earth, awakening memories within us.

AMBLYGONITE

Classification:	Phosphate
Colour:	White/greyish, light yellow, pink or lilac
Hardness:	5.5–6
Lustre:	Vitreous to greasy
Rarity:	Relatively common
Found:	Sweden, France, Western Australia, Brazil, USA
Healing attributes:	Calms the soul

Formed in coarse-grained igneous rocks in short, prismatic crystals, amblygonite is a rare mineral which was first discovered in Saxony, Germany in 1817, but occurs in many places around the world. Its name comes from the Greek, amblus for blunt, and gouia for angle, because of the shallow angles of its crystal cleavage. It usually forms large masses, but is often hard to distinguish from the minerals such as quartz or albite that surround it. As it contains lithium, however, powdered amblygonite will burn red.

A transparent to translucent, delicately coloured stone, amblygonite has an affinity for both the solar plexus and heart chakras. The high lithium content also make it helpful for those suffering from depression, and it encourages a more optimistic outlook on life. It soothes and calms, removing anger and irritation and filling the solar plexus with peace and contentment.

AMETHYST

Classification:	Silicate
Colour:	Purple
Hardness:	7
Lustre:	Vitreous or resinous
Rarity:	Common
Found:	Russia, Namibia, South Africa, Brazil, Canada, USA
Healing attributes:	Protects against psychic attacks, affinity with brow and crown chakras

One of the most distinctive crystals, amethyst is a purple form of quartz and occurs all over the planet. Small traces of iron in the quartz give amethyst a violet colour, which ranges from lilac to deep purple, and it is usually found in places where granite is exposed. Some of the largest crystals have been found in Brazil, where they formed in huge geodes – some large enough to walk though.

The word amethyst is believed to derive from the Greek amethustos, meaning non-inebriated; traditionally amethyst was supposed to protect the wearer from drunkenness. The name may originate in the Greek myth about Dionysius, the god of wine. Tired and emotional after a night of revelling and angered by a human, Dionysius swore that a tiger would eat the next person that crossed his path. A beautiful girl named Amethyst happened to be that unfortunate person, but before Dionysius could carry out his vow, the goddess Athene turned her into a crystal statue. Ashamed by his anger and amazed by Athene's miracle, Dionysius wept into his wine goblet at the feet of the statue. The wine overflowed and turned the statue purple. The belief that amethyst would ward off inebriation persisted, and it was not only worn as an amulet, but was also carved into goblets and drinking vessels.

149

One legend stated that amethyst could control wicked thoughts, and in the middle ages it came to represent celibacy and piety. Amethyst was a popular stone with Christians and it became associated with bishops, whose rings of office are often made from amethyst.

Highly prized and possessed of a powerful force, amethyst is a valuable healing stone with an especial affinity for the brow and crown chakras. It has the ability to awaken and activate spiritual awareness and psychic abilities. A popular stone for meditation, it encourages a calmness of mind and helps the user to fall into a deep meditative state, when they may discover inner wisdom. It is sometimes said that it brings us to the peace which passes all understanding.

As a stone of tranquillity and contentment, amethyst is excellent for relieving stress and strain, and soothing anger, balancing mood swings and dispelling fear and negativity. It is also a powerful stone of protection and guards against psychic attack, protecting the wearer from all types of harm. With its ability to clear negative and

blocked energy, an amethyst cluster provides a valuable and calming addition to any room. Partly because of its traditional associations with sobriety, amethyst is a useful stone for anyone trying to relieve themselves of an addiction, be it to alcohol, drugs, or anything else. It is also useful for treating problems of the skeletal system, for reducing swellings and bruising, and for alleviating respiratory, digestive and skin problems, along with disorders of the heart and circulation, hearing and teeth. It may also be placed under the pillow to relieve insomnia and prevent nightmares.

AMETRINE

Classification:	Silicate
Colour:	Purple and yellow
Hardness:	6
Lustre:	Vitreous to greasy
Rarity:	Extremely rare
Found:	Bolivia
Healing attributes:	Eases change, soothes allergies

Naturally occurring ametrine is only found in eastern Bolivia; it is an amalgam of amethyst and citrine, which are both forms of quartz whose colour derives from iron minerals. Small amounts of citrine have been found in amethysts from India and Brazil, but ametrine has recently been synthetically produced in Russia.

An unusual and beautiful stone, ametrine incorporates the qualities of both citrine and amethyst. The purple colour gives it an affinity for the crown chakra, while the yellow associates it with the solar plexus. It is an excellent meditation stone, enabling one to connect with one's spirituality, opening up intuition and bringing forth creativity and inspiration.

Ametrine can help soothe troubled souls by dissolving emotional blockages, calming the emotions and dispelling negativity. It can help instigate change and ease transition, making it useful for teenagers during puberty, or when changes of partner, job or home are on the horizon. Ametrine also has the power to alleviate allergies, physical, mental and emotional exhaustion and digestive disorders.

AQUAMARINE

Classification: Silicate

Colour: Sea green/light blue

Hardness: 7–8

Lustre: Vitreous

Rarity: Widely available

Found: Ireland, Russia, USA, Mexico, Brazil, Afghanistant, Pakistan, India, Zimbabwe

Healing attributes: Cleanses the throat chakra, heightens spiritual sensitivity

A semi-precious stone, aquamarine is a form of beryl. Its light blue-green tones are reminiscent of the sea, and its name is the Latin for seawater. Because of its colour, it has always had maritime associations, and was traditionally thought to protect sailors from drowning. In legends, aquamarine appears as mermaid treasure.

Aquamarine is a harmonizing stone that cleanse the throat chakra and allows us to speak the truth. It promotes courage, enabling us to face up to situations and to stand our ground. It also increases spiritual awareness and is useful as a meditation aid because it calms the mind while at the same time improving mental clarity.

Aquamarine soothes physical manifestations such as rashes, allergies or swollen glands and may be placed over tired eyes or inflamed glands.

AVENTURINE

Classification:	Silicate
Colour:	Varies from mid-blue, to brownish-red to grey and yellow. Most commonly sea green
Hardness:	7
Lustre:	Vitreous
Rarity:	Widely available
Found:	Italy, Austria, Brazil, India, Tibet, Nepal, Russia, China
Healing attributes:	Heart problems, relaxation

The opaque aventurine derives its name from the Italian a ventura, meaning ' by chance' or 'random'. Whether this is because of its chance discovery, or because of the random distribution of tiny shiny mica particles within the stones remains open to debate. It is regarded as a positive stone, bringing prosperity and luck, and dispelling environmental pollution, such as that emanating from cell phones and computers.

It is associated with the heart chakra, which it clears and protects, and is generally useful for treating heart problems: not only does it strengthen and stabilise the heart, but it also encourages regeneration. Aventurine can also help alleviate lung and throat disorders, insomnia, allergies and skin diseases.

Aventurine encourages feelings of deep relaxation and contentment, filling the heart with love and joy, so it is excellent for those who feel unloved or who find it hard to open their hearts, to trust and form close relationships.

AZEZTULITE

Classification:	Silicate
Colour:	Colourless or white
Hardness:	7
Lustre:	Vitreous or resinous.
Rarity:	Extremely rare
Found:	North Carolina
Healing attributes:	Inflammation, cancer

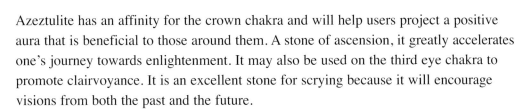

A rare quartz crystal found only in one mine in North Carolina, USA, azeztulite has an extremely high frequency and crystal therapists believe that it is one of those exceptional stones that never needs to be cleansed or energised. It is believed to have a powerful vibration that provides a mystical connection to the angelic realm.

Azeztulite has an affinity for the crown chakra and will help users project a positive aura that is beneficial to those around them. A stone of ascension, it greatly accelerates one's journey towards enlightenment. It may also be used on the third eye chakra to promote clairvoyance. It is an excellent stone for scrying because it will encourage visions from both the past and the future.

It is a remarkable crystal that has also been used to treat inflammatory disorders and cancer.

AZURITE

Classification:	Hydrated carbonate
Colour:	Light to dark blue
Hardness:	3.5–4
Lustre:	Vitreous to dull
Rarity:	Often found near malachite
Found:	France, Morocco, Egypt, China, Australia, USA, Peru
Healing attributes:	Throat chakra, rheumatism

The striking deep blue crystals of azurite are formed by the weathering of copper minerals within the stone: it derives its basic colour from copper, but the presence of water helps turn it bright blue. The stone produces such a pure blue pigment that the Egyptians used it for cosmetic purposes and it was also used as dye for centuries. Medieval and Renaissance painters used it as a source of blue pigment and it was sometimes confused with lapis lazuli. Native Americans regarded it as a sacred stone and believed that it facilitated contact with their spirit guides, while the Mayans used it to heighten their psychic powers.

Azurite is especially beneficial for the throat chakra and for activating the third eye or brow chakra.

Some healers believe that it helps to cure rheumatism – possibly because of its close connection with copper. It is also useful in the treatment of spinal disorders and circulatory complaints, as well as liver, gallbladder, thyroid and throat problems.

BERYL

Classification:	Silicate
Colour:	Colourless, yellowish, green, red, gold, pink
Hardness:	7.5–8
Lustre:	Vitreous to resinous
Rarity:	Widely available
Found:	Spain, Russia, Namibia, Madagascar Pakistan, Colombia, Brazil, USA
Healing attributes:	Increases confidence, soothes heart or liver problems

Beryl is often referred to as the 'mother of gemstones' because it has many attractive varieties, famously emerald and aquamarine which are chemically and structurally identical. It is a relatively common mineral and when pure has absolutely no colour; colour variations are the result of trace metallic elements within the stone, which give it a rich colour palette. Beryl has small, six-sided prismatic crystals, although some huge examples measuring up to 5.5m (18 ft) have been found in Colombia.

In healing, beryl helps to focus the mind, decluttering it by removing transitory distractions and encouraging positive thinking. It is one of the strongest crystals for dealing with anxiety and helps users to find true spiritual guidance.

Golden beryl

In its yellow or golden form, beryl was sometimes regarded as a crystal of the sun, and can be used as an antidote for liver disorders. It is a valuable stone for scrying and is sometimes used in ritual magic. It promotes confidence, independence and initiative and opens up the crown and solar plexus chakras.

See also emerald, aquamarine and morganite.

BLOODSTONE (or heliotrope)

Classification:	Silicate
Colour:	Dark green/grey, flecked red
Hardness:	7
Lustre:	Vitreous or resinous
Rarity:	Common
Found:	India, Australia, USA
Healing attributes:	Blood disorders, reduces infection

Bloodstone is a variety of opaque dark green chalcedony that is flecked with red spots. It has been regarded as a healing stone for centuries, and its alternative name, heliotrope, comes from the Greek helio, meaning solstice – highly polished examples were used to reflect the sun. The stone is also referred to as green or blood jasper. It was a valuable stone in medieval times, when Christians believed that it was first formed when drops of Christ's blood fell from his body on the cross and stained a piece of jasper. It was frequently used to carve representations of the crucifixion and became known as the 'martyrs' stone'.

Bloodstone will alleviate both physical and emotional problems associated with the heart, making it an invaluable crystal for those who have trouble establishing strong and lasting relationships. Traditionally used to treat blood disorders, powdered bloodstone is still used as a medicine and as an aphrodisiac in India today. It purifies and fortifies the blood, making it ideal for anaemia, and is one of the most effective stones for boosting the immune system.

It should be placed on the thymus gland above the heart for optimum effect. It reduces pus formation, neutralizes toxins and stimulates the lymphatic system, so is highly recommended for reducing infection and inflammation.

158

BOJI® STONE

Classification:	Mineraloid
Colour:	Dark grey, brown
Hardness:	7.4
Lustre:	Dull
Rarity:	Rare
Found:	Kansas, USA
Healing attributes:	Restores equilibrium, grounds individuals

Brown to blackish stones, true Boji stones originate in Kansas, where their power was discovered by the young Karen Gillespie, who named them after her pet crow, Boji. With high levels of iron magnetite and pyrites, smooth, rounded stones emit female energy, whereas more uneven specimens are regarded as male. They are excellent stones for the base chakra and when used for grounding will dispel any feelings of 'spaciness'.

Bojis have exceptional balancing and healing abilities and for this reason are usually sold in pairs. Hold a pair (one male, one female) in each hand for ten to 20 minutes to stimulate the acupuncture meridians and dissolve physical and emotional blockages. Many people report feeling a mild tingling or electrical charge as energy blockages are removed.
If you carry a pair around with you, they will provide continuous protection and balancing energy, which will cleanse and charge your aura.

CALCITE

Classification:	Carbonate
Colour:	Colourless, red, yellow, gold, green, blue
Hardness:	3
Lustre:	Vitreous to resinous to dull
Rarity:	Extremely common
Found:	UK, Belgium, Iceland, USA, Brazil, India, Germany
Healing attributes:	Intellectual development; dispels negativity

Calcite (calcium carbonate) is one of the world's most common minerals and the crystals, which form in fissures and pockets of basalt (and other) rocks, are colourless until combined with certain trace metals. There are over 300 different types of calcite crystals and they appear in a veritable rainbow of colours; their colour symbolism is critical to their use in crystal therapy.

In general, calcite will dispel negative energies and recharge the environment around you. On a personal level it will revive emotional intelligence, and improve motivation; it is especially useful for students as it encourages intellectual growth and improves the retention of knowledge.

Blue calcite
Soothing blue calcite has an affinity for the throat chakra and is excellent for healing throat inflammation, as well as lung and thyroid disorders. It is a superb stone for reducing stress, anxiety and negativity, as well as regulating blood pressure.

160

Green calcite

Green calcite is related to the heart chakra and the nervous system. It stimulates the thymus gland, helping the body to conquer infections and boosting the immune system. Because it is able to absorb negative vibes, green calcite should always be thoroughly cleansed after use.

Orange calcite

Orange calcite tunes in with the sacral chakra and the abdomen and is recommended for all problems relating to the reproductive system, particularly loss of libido. It is also effective in the treatment of digestive problems such as constipation or irritable bowel syndrome. It is an energising stone and will help remove fear and conquer depression.

Red calcite

An uplifting and energising stone, red calcite increases vitality and zest for life. It will reduce lower back pain, sciatica and treat problems related to the hips, legs and knees. Red calcite is also used to treat the reproductive organs, because it has special powers to cleanse and stimulate the genitals. It may also be used to deal with problems of infertility.

CARNELIAN

Classification:	Silicate
Colour:	Orange, red-brown, pink
Hardness:	7
Lustre:	Vitreous or resinous
Rarity:	Common
Found:	India, Australia, Brazil, Britain, Iceland
Healing attributes:	Revitalizes the metabolism, improves fertility

Carnelian is a type of chalcedony that gains its red/orange colour from the presence of iron. The smooth, translucent appearance of the stone is typical of chalcedony, which is formed at low temperatures in volcanic cavities and consequently has small crystals. Chalcedony is one of the most widely used gems throughout history, and it is likely that it was one of the first hard materials to be fashioned into tools by Palaeolithic man. The Egyptians revered the power of carnelian, believing that it eased the passage to the afterlife. It was used by several cultures to make signet rings: the Greeks and Romans valued it, and Moslems believe that carving the name of Allah on to carnelian boosts courage. Native Americans believed it promoted stability and harmony and used it as a sacred stone.

Healers use carnelian to boost fertility and stimulate sexuality, as it is especial useful for the sacral and base chakras. It is especially useful to those who struggle to express their sexuality. It is excellent for raising energy levels and spurring the lethargic into action. Carnelian has the ability to stimulate the brain, clearing the mind of confusion and improving concentration and problem-solving.

Fiery carnelian is a stone of courage and helps us to stand up for what we believe in. It helps to banish negative emotions such as fear and depression, and in this way protects and uplifts the user. It offers powerful protection against fear and resentment and calms anger. It can also be used to cleanse other stones.

Carnelian is recommended for treating disorders of the blood and circulation and aids the absorption of vitamins and minerals.

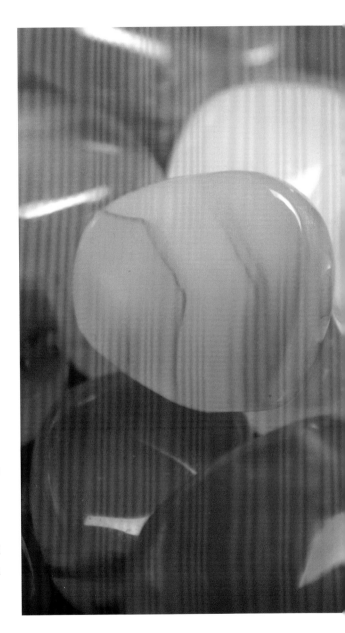

CHAROITE

Classification:	Silicate
Colour:	Purple
Hardness:	5
Lustre:	Vitreous to pearly
Rarity:	Very rare
Found:	Russia
Healing attributes:	Cleansing, promotes peaceful sleep

The unmistakeable lilac or purple swirls of charoite are found in only one location – along the banks of the River Chary at Alden in Russia. It is a product of a unique set of geological circumstances in the limestone-rich environment of the river.

Rare crystals often encourage dreaming, and charoite is no exception. It is a magical and mysterious stone with the ability to transform and manifest our dreams and aspirations. It is a stone of prophecy and assists in interpreting our visions.

It is a cleanser and can be a stone of transformation, dispelling negative energy to clear auras and chakras by turning negative forces into positive vibes. It enables us to express our unconditional love by opening our hearts. Children are often drawn to this stone, perhaps because it allays nightmares and encourages peaceful sleep. It can also treat disorders of the eye, heart, liver and pancreas, as well as banishing headaches and alleviating aches and pains.

CHRYSOCOLLA

Classification:	Silicate
Colour:	Green, blue/green
Hardness:	2–4
Lustre:	Vitreous
Rarity:	Relatively common
Found:	USA, Israel, Zaire, UK
Healing attributes:	Inflammation, self-awareness, natural harmonies

Chrysocolla usually occurs in the earth near copper deposits and its translucent greenish colour is an important marker for ore prospectors. Pure chrysocolla is actually a mineraloid – it does not have a crystalline structure and is soft and fragile. However, at high temperatures it can be 'agatized' and merges with chalcedony to form harder quartz stones that sparkle with a layer of fine quartz crystals. Its name is derived from the Greek chrysos, meaning gold, and kola, meaning glue.

In healing terms, chrysocolla is aligned with the throat chakra and can treat infections and inflammations of the sinuses, tonsils, larynx and lungs. Its affinity with the throat chakra also means that it is excellent for improving communication and encouraging self-awareness and inner strength.

A cooling stone, chrysocolla soothes all types of inflammation, from sunburn to irritable bowel syndrome, and will help detoxify the liver, kidneys and other organs. It has the power to regulate the nervous system and pancreas, as well as levels of blood sugar, so is an excellent crystal for diabetics.

CHRYSOPRASE

Classification:	Silicate
Colour:	Bright green
Hardness:	7
Lustre:	Vitreous or resinous
Rarity:	Fairly common
Found:	Australia, Russia, USA, Brazil
Healing attributes:	Relationships, detoxifiying

Chrysoprase is the rarest and most valuable of the chalcedony stones, highly sought-after for its brilliant apple-green colour, which is produced by traces of nickel. It was a popular jewel from ancient Egyptian times, and the Greeks and Romans often cut it into cameos. Mined extensively in Silesia, it decorates many buildings in eastern Europe, including the Wenceslas Chapel in Prague. Today most chrysoprase comes from Australia.

According to the 11th century Byzantine manuscript of Michael Psellius, chrysoprase was meant to strengthen vision and relieve internal pain. Healers today know that it has an especial affinity for the heart chakra, and can help mend a broken heart or revive a relationship. It energises and transforms grief, envy, greed and jealousy into positive emotions, and promotes forgiveness.

A detoxifying stone, chrysoprase aids waste elimination from the body and mind; it stimulates the liver and rids the psyche of poisons by promoting an open mind. Its calming influence will improve sleep patterns and it is ideal for children who suffer from nightmares. It encourages feelings of security and has been used to dispel feelings of claustrophobia.

CITRINE

Classification:	Silicate
Colour:	Yellow (pale to golden brown)
Hardness:	7
Lustre:	Vitreous or resinous
Rarity:	Scarce
Found:	Spain, Russia, France, Madagascar, Brazil
Healing attributes:	Energising, promotes prosperity and generosity

Citrine derives its name from citrus, the Latin for yellow, and its colour from tiny particles of iron oxide within quartz – it is simply a yellow form of quartz. Having said that, it is probably the most highly valued quartz gem, and is sometimes mistaken for topaz. Pure citrine is comparatively rare, although it can be artificially produced by heat-treating amethyst, which produces a deeper orange colour crystal.

Its brilliant yellow colour is naturally energising and matches that of the third or solar plexus chakra, which it cleanses and balances. It will promote self-confidence and encourage generosity.

Citrine is marvellous for stimulating the brain and strengthening the intellect: it enhances creativity and the generation of new ideas and helps with problem-solving. It is also known as a stone of abundance and prosperity (probably because of its golden colour) and helps users to acquire wealth and then to keep it.

Citrine is an ideal crystal for those who feel tired and drained and are in need of an energy boost. Its affinity with the solar plexus chakra also means that it will benefit the kidneys, bladder, stomach, pancreas and spleen.

DANBURITE

Classification:	Silicate
Colour:	Colourless, white, rose, yellow, lilac
Hardness:	7
Lustre:	Vitreous
Rarity:	Widely available
Found:	USA. Russia, Japan, Mexico, Myanmar
Healing attributes:	Powerful healing stone

First discovered in 1839, in Danbury, Connecticut, danburite is usually a perfectly clear crystal with a wedge-shaped termination, in contrast to the pyramidal termination of quartz, for example.

Danburite is a spiritual stone and is associated with the crown chakra; it can act as a bridge to higher planes of consciousness and the angelic realms. Wearers often feel more serene and more in touch with their spiritual selves. Danburite carries a very high vibration, which allows users to attain higher states of spirituality and eases them along the path to enlightenment. It is an excellent stone for releasing karma and helping people to make changes. Placed by the bedside of a dying person, it will help them on their journey to another world.

Danburite will effectively balance the right and left sides of the brain and will help release blockages in the acupuncture meridians. It clears allergies and removes toxins, and is especially useful in relation to the liver and gallbladder.

DIAMOND

Classification: Element

Colour: Colourless, sometimes tinged with yellow, blue, brown or pink

Hardness: 10

Lustre: Adamantine (greasy when rough)

Rarity: Rare (hence expensive)

Found: South Africa, Russia, Brazil, Australia, USA

Healing attributes: Purification and detoxification; affinity for the crown chakra; its clarity means it is good for visual problems.

Diamond is pure carbon and almost the hardest substance on Earth (only lonsdaleite, the mineral formed in meteorite impacts, is harder). Great pressure on carbon underground produces the sparkling stones that are so highly prized the world over. Such pressure is rare in nature and occurs deep within the Earth's crust and upper mantle, some 90 miles (145 km) below the surface. Incredibly, the diamonds found today are at least a billion years old and were carried to the surface up volcanic pipes of hot magma which cooled to form rocks known as kimberlites and lamproites.

Pliny called diamonds 'the substance that possesses the greatest value, not only among the precious stones, but of all human possessions' and knew that its hardness was 'beyond all expression'. Diamonds may appear rather greasy when excavated, and it was not until the 15th century that jewellers acquired the means to cut and polish them into the facets that we recognise today; only then did people recognise the acute brilliance of the stone. They remain the most highly valued gems on earth and have endowed royal regalia from Biblical times. The largest diamond ever found emerged in South Africa in 1907, weighing 3,106 carats (1.3 lb). Known as the Cullinan Diamond, it was presented to Edward VII of Great Britain. It was cut into four, with one piece, the 530-carat Star of Africa set in the British sovereign's sceptre. A second piece, Cullinan II is set in the Imperial State Crown.

Known as the 'king of crystals', diamonds are the only stones that do not need to be recharged in crystal therapy. It is a symbol of purity, and its energizing white light has an immediate affinity with the crown chakra. Diamond links us to the divine and removes obstacles blocking the pathway to enlightenment. They are excellent for cleansing negativity from the aura.

Diamonds have long been regarded as tokens of love and lasting bonds; they help to establish a strong and lasting relationship, encouraging trust, fidelity and perseverance.

A stone that works to clear the mind, diamonds enable one to see the correct course of action very clearly; diamonds acutely reflect the strengths and weaknesses of any problem. It can also be used to treat dizziness and vertigo effectively. Diamonds may additionally be used to purify and detoxify all of the body's systems, to build up stamina. strength and fearlessness, and to treat chronic conditions.

EMERALD

Classification:	Silicate
Colour:	Green
Hardness:	7.5–8
Lustre:	Vitreous
Rarity:	Rare
Found:	Colombia, Egypt, India, Zimbabwe, Pakistan, Brazil, Madagascar, Russia
Healing attributes:	Problems of the heart, eye disorders

Emerald is a form of beryl that contains traces of chromium and vanadium, which give the stone its rich green colour. The name is derived from the Greek, smaragdos, meaning green, and they are one of the oldest gems known to mankind. Emeralds are mentioned in the Bible – an emerald was included in the breastplate of Aaron, the Jewish high priest – and in the Hindu Vedas scriptures, which note that the precious gems 'promise good luck'…and 'enhance well-being'. In Roman times, the Emperor Nero apparently used emeralds like sunglasses, looking through one to watch gladiatorial combat. In the middle ages, emeralds were reputed to have miraculous powers, such as the ability to preserve or heal the sight.

The best specimens have come from South America (and many were plundered by the Spanish conquistadors of the 16th century), but in ancient times, emeralds were mined in Egypt and India. In the 19th century, two ancient mines were excavated in Egypt, including one that became known as 'Cleopatra's Mine' near the Red Sea. One of the largest emeralds ever found was mined in Colombia in the 1920s. Known as the Patricia Emerald it weighed 632 carats.

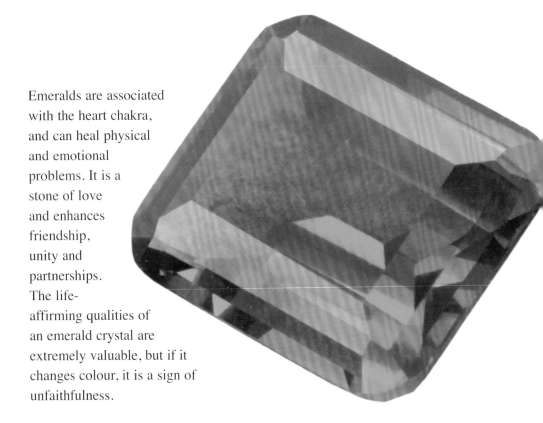

Emeralds are associated with the heart chakra, and can heal physical and emotional problems. It is a stone of love and enhances friendship, unity and partnerships. The life-affirming qualities of an emerald crystal are extremely valuable, but if it changes colour, it is a sign of unfaithfulness.

Emeralds improve mental clarity, stimulate the brain and enhance the memory, helping us to make the right decisions. It is an excellent stone for meditation, partly because of it relaxing green colour, which facilitates deep breathing, relaxing the shoulders, upper back and chest.

Highly beneficial in the treatment of eye disorders, an emerald can be placed in a bowl of water over night. Soak cotton wool pads in the emerald elixir and place them over your closed eyes to revive them. Emeralds can also be used to treat spinal problems, muscular aches, skin ulcers, weak immune systems, liver complaints and toxic conditions.

FLUORITE

Classification:	Salt
Colour:	Wide variety, from clear to black, via purple, blue, green, yellow, reddish, pink, white, brown
Hardness:	4
Lustre:	Vitreous
Rarity:	Common
Found:	England, Germany, Italy, Switzerland, Russia, India, USA, Mexico
Healing attributes:	Psychic protection, cell regeneration

Known to geologists as the most colourful mineral in the world, fluorite's range of colours is rivalled only by those of quartz. Fluorite is a versatile mineral, which can be found around the world, with colours ranging from purple, black, and blue, through magenta and green, to yellow, pink and white.

Originally named fluorspar by the German mineralogist Georg Agricola in 1546, the name derives from the Latin fluere, meaning to flow, because fluorite melts easily. In fact, it has been used since Roman times as flux – a material that lowers the melting point of another substance to make it easier to work; it is still used in the steel and aluminium industries today. It is also the source of all fluorine used today – including the fluorine in your toothpaste. Clear fluorite has excellent optical capabilities and is sometimes used in the manufacture of microscope lenses because it eliminates colour distortion. The word fluorescent (the light emitted by a material when exposed to ultraviolet rays) derives from fluorite, which was one of the first materials studied, and indeed, did not disappoint. In addition to glowing blue, green or purple, like most materials under UV light, fluorite can also glow white, red or violet, probably because it contains traces of uranium and rare-earth metals within it.

As befits a crystal that is so extraordinary in scientific terms, fluorite is an exceptional defensive stone on a psychic level. It offers effective protection against electromagnetic pollution from mobile phones and computers, and can counter geopathic stress created by negative ley lines. The colour of the stone will determine which chakra is most effectively balanced: purple fluorite for the brow chakra; green or pink for the heart; blue for the throat, and colourless fluorite for the crown chakra.

It stimulates the regeneration of cells within the body, particularly in the skin and respiratory tract, and stimulates the immune system. Ulcers, cuts, cankers and sores will all benefit from exposure to fluorite, because it is a stone that discourages chaotic, disordered growth. Fluorite is also used to improve skeletal mobility, and blue fluorite, in particular, will reduce inflammation from rheumatoid arthritis, for example.

Fluorite generally has a harmonising effect on the body because it is able to balance the nervous system, while bringing peace and stability to relationships. Purple fluorite is a wonderful stone for meditation, as it improves focus and opens up the intuition, allowing one to see through psychic manipulation and illusion.

177

GARNET

Classification:	Silicate
Colour:	Red, black, yellow, orange, green, grey, colourless (rare)
Hardness:	6.5–7
Lustre:	Vitreous
Rarity:	Abundant
Found:	Worldwide
Healing attributes:	Purification, heart, commitment

Garnets are a group of silicate minerals that occur abundantly around the earth. The most well known are red semi-precious stones, which were called carbuncles in Biblical times, although the name garnet was bestowed by the Greeks because the stones reminded them of pomegranate seeds. In legends garnet is often associated with fire and light. Noah is said to have hung a garnet in the ark to illuminate it, and in India, people once rubbed garnets on their clothes to provide illumination. Garnets have been found in many Scandinavian graves, where they were placed to light the path to the afterlife.

A crystal of purification, regeneration and warmth, garnet is affiliated to the base chakra in healing, where it breaks down blockages and stimulates the kundalini (our untapped creative energy). Garnet also grounds us, making us feel safe and secure. It boosts confidence and provides the courage to face problematic situations and crises. It helps build strength of character and enhances inner strength and certainty, especially in the face of change.

It is an excellent stone for stimulating the circulation and strengthening the heart. Garnet is often used in relation to blood disorders and can boost the immune system and energy levels.

Garnet is a stone of love and commitment that brings warmth and devotion, understanding and trust, sincerity and honesty to a relationship.

HAEMATITE

Classification:	Oxide
Colour:	Steel grey to black, red to brown
Hardness:	5–6
Lustre:	Metallic/dull
Rarity:	Abundant
Found:	England, Switzerland, Italy, Australia, Brazil, Canada
Healing attributes:	Grounding, treats anaemia

Haematite is the world's most important iron ore and is a vital mineral to the economies of many countries. A shiny stone, it is relatively heavy, because of its high iron content (70%). It has probably been used since earliest times, first as a tool and then for decorative or spiritual purposes. The ancient Egyptians used haematite in their amulets and ancient people believed that haematite formed on battlefields from the blood of fallen warriors. The name comes from the Greek, haem, meaning blood and the Romans believed it bestowed a protective power during battle. In his Naturalis Historia, Pliny wrote that haematite was a powerful talisman, which could secure a favourable outcome in legal judgements. Haematite was ground down to produce the dye red ochre, which Native American tribes used as a face paint, and in medieval times it was used to staunch blood flow and treat wounds.

Haematite is related to the base chakra and therefore strengthens our connection with the earth, promoting stability, security, strength and courage. It will not only dissipate negative energy, but also prevents the absorption of negative influences from the environment around you.

It is a calming stone that will soothe nerves and can be used to alleviate insomnia, stress and anxiety. Haematite is a useful stone to apply at the end of a treatment if you feel slightly light-headed and ungrounded. Haematite will help you to retain your cool – both physically and mentally – so try placing it on you forehead to reduce fever, or on to any inflamed part of the body.

Given its traditional associations with blood, it is no surprise that haematite can be used to treat anaemia; it may also improve the quality of the blood and reduce blood pressure. It is recommended during childbirth, both to reduce blood loss and to calm everyone in the delivery suite. Sufferers of arthritis, leg cramps and other musculo-skeletal conditions may find that placing a haematite stone under their pillow brings relief.

IOLITE

Classification:	Silicate
Colour:	Blue-violet
Hardness:	7–7.5
Lustre:	Vitreous
Rarity:	Reasonably common
Found:	Brazil, USA, Sri Lanka, Madagascar
Healing attributes:	Reduces fatty deposits, third eye healing

A variety of the mineral cordierite, iolite appears to change colour – the colour alters when the stone is viewed from different angles, a feature known as pleochroism. It is most commonly an attractive violet-blue colour, and is sometimes referred to as 'water-sapphire', although it may also appear blue, grey, green or brown. The name derives from the Greek, ios meaning violet, and the Vikings used it as the world's first polarizing lens on their legendary voyages of discovery – it enabled them to determine the direction of the sun on overcast days sun and navigate accordingly.

Iolite has an affinity for the brow chakra and increases one's perception. It is a stone of visions and has been used in shamanic healing ceremonies to enhance the gift of prophecy. It can awaken psychic abilities when used in meditation.

Iolite can be used to detoxify and rid the body of fatty deposits, dispersing the effects of alcohol by purifying the liver. It is a useful stone for curing addictions, enabling the user to free themselves from the expectations imposed by those around them.

JADE

Classification:	Silicate
Colour:	Green
Hardness:	Jadeite 6.5–7; nephrite 5.5–6
Lustre:	Vitreous, dull
Rarity:	Rare, although nephrite is more widely available
Found:	Russia, China, Burma, Japan, USA, Central America
Healing attributes:	Heart chakra, kidney problems

Jade is the popular name given to two minerals, the very rare and highly valued jadeite, which was long cherished in China and the Far East, and the more commonly occurring and softer nephrite, which is found in South America, China and New Zealand among other localities. Maoris made nephrite into ornaments and jewellery, but the most highly prized jade is that from China, where it was a symbol of royalty and has been fashioned into jewellery and ornaments for centuries. Fine-graded jadeite is tougher than steel, so it is not surprising that the Aztec and Inca peoples of South America used it to make knives and axes. Jadeite is generally a darker, richer green than nephrite, although in its purest form it is white. It was traditionally worn as a stone of good fortune and in South America was regarded as effective against kidney infections. (The word jade derives from the Spanish piedra de ijada, meaning stone of the side.)

Green jade (and the less common lavender variety) are both sympathetic to the heart chakra. Physically, jade will deepen the breathing and strengthen the heart, while emotionally it encourages compassion and the establishment of strong bonds. Jade is a stone of stability and will dispel mood swings and calm anger and irritability. Excellent for kidney problems, it also balances the metabolism as a whole.

Jade is a valuable dream stone, and if a piece is placed under the pillow, it will encourage the dreamer both to remember and to interpret their dreams. It has long been regarded as a stone of wisdom and assists in decision-making.

JASPER

Classification:	Silicate
Colour:	Green, red, yellow, brown, blue, purple, black
Hardness:	7
Lustre:	Vitreous or resinous
Rarity:	Common
Found:	Worldwide
Healing attributes:	Nurturing

In its natural environment jasper, a form of chalcedony, is a dull stone, but once polished, it is a glistening, opaque crystal whose colour ranges from red, to brownish, yellow to green. The name is derived from the Greek iaspis, meaning spotted stone and it was widely known in ancient times. Many scholars believe it was the stone named as yashepheh in Exodus and noted as the 12th stone in the breastplate of the Jewish high priest, which represented the tribe of Benjamin. Used for making amulets in ancient Egypt, it was also revered by shamans as a sacred and protective stone. It was widely used in the 16th century in mosaic work, particularly the commesso or Florentine mosaic. Some Native American tribes referred to it as the ' rain-bringer' and interestingly, it had a similar name in early medieval Europe.

Jasper is sometimes called the 'supreme nurturer', because it counters stress and brings tranquillity to the whole person. Jasper is found in several different colours and can be used in chakra layouts, with each stone relevant to a specific chakra.

Green jasper harmonises the heart chakra. As well as helping to boost the immune system and detoxifiying all the body's systems, it protects against pollution.

Red jasper balances and grounds the base chakra, bestowing courage and the willpower to achieve one's goals. Excellent for stimulating the circulation and increasing energy, red jasper is a nurturing stone that is helpful in times of convalescence. It may also be used to treat sexual problems and disorders of the intestines.

Yellow jasper balances the solar plexus chakra, calms the nerves and is a useful protective stone, especially against jealousy. It also alleviates disorders of the stomach and relieves bloating.

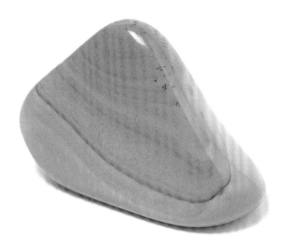

Black jasper grounds the base chakra and is good for absorbing anger or coping with repressed feelings. It is also a good scrying stone and encourages prophetic dreams.

KUNZITE

Classification: Silicate

Colour: Pink/lilac

Hardness: 6.5–7.5

Lustre: Vitreous

Rarity: Uncommon

Found: USA, Brazil, Canada, Russia, Mexico, Sweden

Healing attributes: Heart chakra, meditation, panic attacks

A lilac form of spodumene, kunzite is named after the renowned gem expert Dr George F Kunz who discovered it in Connecticut in 1902. Spodumene crystals can be huge – some have been found in the Black Hills of South Dakota nearly 15m (50ft) long, and weighing 90 tonnes. The delicate colour of kunzite is caused by the presence of manganese in the rock.

Kunzite has an affinity for the heart chakra, and also aligns it with the throat and third eye chakras. Kunzite is a stone of love and peace, connecting us with the compassion and peace of the Divine Being. It is a stone which can comfort and heal the heart on both physical and emotional levels, and is especially useful for those who find it difficult to express their emotions and bond with those around them. It encourages the qualities of forgiveness and selfless devotion.

A protective stone that shields the user against negative or unwanted energies, kunzite is excellent for use in meditation. With the ability to raise spiritual vibrations, it allows one to reach a higher state of spiritual awareness and enhances the intuition. Kunzite exudes purity and innocence and is a good stone for children and babies, who gain a sense of security from it.

Kunzite is also useful for dispersing panic attacks and relieving stress and tension, as well as treating lung disease, circulatory problems, sciatica, neuralgia and hormonal problems.

LAPIS LAZULI

Classification:	Silicate
Colour:	Blue
Hardness:	5.5–6
Lustre:	Greasy to dull
Rarity:	Uncommon
Found:	Afghanistan, Siberia, Chile, USA, Italy
Healing attributes:	Throat problems, communication, sleep problems

Allegedly presented to humankind by angels, the striking blue of lapis lazuli has been prized for centuries. The name derives from several sources: from the Persian lazar, meaning blue, and the Latin lapis, meaning stone. The ancient Egyptians used it in their temples because they believed it was a stone from heaven – the midnight blue colour is like that of the night sky, and the golden flecks of pyrite resemble the stars. It decorates the tomb of Tutankhamen and the ancient Sumerian tombs of Ur, and it was traded throughout the Mesopotamia and Mediterranean region. Mined in Afghanistan (still the source of the finest lapis), it was introduced to Europe by Alexander the Great, when it became known as ultramarine, literally meaning 'from beyond the seas'. The Roman writer Pliny called it 'a fragment of the starry firmament'. For generations artists and painters manufactured ultramarine pigment from crushed lapis, which was extremely expensive, but had a colour that outshone others and has proved to outlast them.

Lapis lazuli is associated with the third eye and with the throat chakra. When placed on the third eye it connects us with the source of omnipotence and reveals inner truths. It heightens and expands sensitivity to the intuitive, encouraging psychic revelations and introducing visions and insights into our dreams. If used on the throat chakra, lapis energises it, and can be used to treat problems of the throat, thyroid, neck, vocal cords, ears, chest and lungs.

Lapis lazuli will dispel repressed anger and help lessen mood swings. It is recommended for those who have trouble in speaking their minds, or expressing their emotions. It endows self-confidence, mental clarity and facilitates easier communication.

It may be worn as a stone of protection to guard against psychic attacks. It has also been used to reduce pain, promoting restful sleep and reducing vertigo and dizziness.

LARIMAR

Classification:	Silicate
Colour:	Blue-white
Hardness:	5–7 (darker stones are harder)
Lustre:	Vitreous
Rarity:	Uncommon
Found:	Dominican Republic
Healing attributes:	Feet, throat

A variety of blue pectolite, larimar was discovered off the coast of the Dominican Republic in 1974 by Miguel Mendez who named it after his daughter Larissa and the sea (mar in Spanish), hence larimar. The beautiful blue-white stones,which seem to reflect the colour of the Caribbean Sea, are only found in the Dominican Republic where their unique volcanic blue colour is highly prized.

Sometimes called the 'dolphin stone' or the 'Atlantis stone', larimar is spiritually empowering and has an affinity for the third eye chakra. It is used as a meditation stone to calm the mind and bestow inner peace. It facilitates contact with the angelic realms and apparently summons past lives from the realm of Atlantis.

Larimar also aligns the throat chakra and can be used to tone and heal the throat and neck. It is a stone of harmony that can balance the yin and yang energies in us. It is excellent for unblocking meridians and dissolving energy blocks, particularly in the throat and chest. This means it will also draw pain out of the body and promote self-healing.

LEPIDOLITE

Classification: Silicate

Colour: Pink, greyish, lilac, white

Hardness: 2.5–3

Lustre: Vitreous

Rarity: Easily obtainable

Found: Brazil, Russia, Germany, USA, Mozambique, Madagascar

Healing attributes: Treats confusion, counters electromagnetic pollution

A translucent or transparent mineral with a pearly or vitreous lustre, lepidolite is often found in tin-rich mineral veins. It is one of the most attractive micas (aluminium silicate minerals with transparent, almost flaky layers) and is a secondary source of lithium.

Healers often refer to it as a peace stone, and it can be used for earth healing as it provides stability for ley lines and tectonic plates. It promotes a calm environment and works to counter electromagnetic radiation.

Lepidolite is especially associated with the third eye and crown chakras, and is an excellent stone for meditation. It can calm the mind, relieve stress and tension, and will help those with disturbed sleep patterns. It aids focus and concentration, encouraging clarity of mind and decision-making. It can be used to treat people with confused minds – the lithium content makes it suitable for those with bipolar disorder. It is also regarded as a stone of change, easing transitions, as well as promoting change in our lives.

MALACHITE

Classification: Carbonate

Colour: Green

Hardness: 3.5–4

Lustre: Vitreous to dull

Rarity: Relatively common

Found: France, Russia, Morocco, Namibia, Australia, USA

Healing attributes: Menstrual pain

Deep-green, banded malachite stones have been tumbled and polished for centuries to be worn as jewellery or used as ornaments. It was widely used and mined in ancient Egypt where it was dedicated to the goddess Hathor, who had dominion over the Sinai Peninsula, the site of the mines. The Romans made it sacred to Venus, and the Vikings associated it with Freya: this widespread association with the primary female goddess meant that malachite became associated with healing women's problems, such as menstruation and labour pains. The ancient Egyptians used ground malachite as eye make-up, partly for decoration, and partly because it was believed to fight eye infections.

Today, healers associate malachite with the heart and throat chakras and use it as a stone of balance to soothe and strengthen the nervous system. Malachite will soothe the heart by drawing out past pain and replace depression with peace and tranquillity. It has the power to bring fidelity to a relationship and loyalty to a friendship.

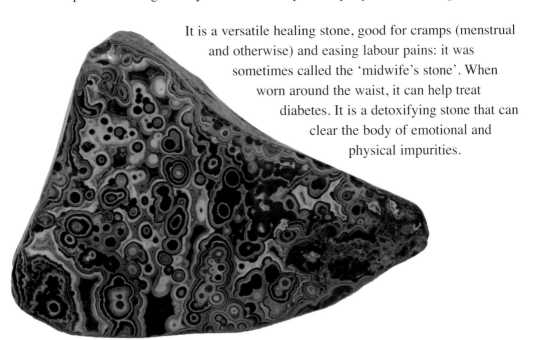

It is a versatile healing stone, good for cramps (menstrual and otherwise) and easing labour pains: it was sometimes called the 'midwife's stone'. When worn around the waist, it can help treat diabetes. It is a detoxifying stone that can clear the body of emotional and physical impurities.

MORGANITE

Classification:	Silicate
Colour:	Rose-pink
Hardness:	7.5–8
Lustre:	Vitreous
Rarity:	Reasonably common
Found:	Afghanistan, Brazil, USA
Healing attributes:	Relaxation

A form of beryl, morganite was simply known as pink beryl until 1911, when the gemstone expert George F Kunz suggested that it deserved the status of a gemstone in its own right, and it was renamed morganite after the noted industrialist and gem collector J P Morgan.

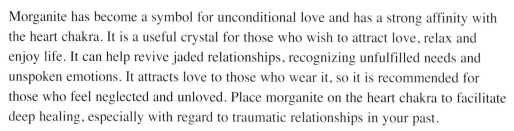

Morganite has become a symbol for unconditional love and has a strong affinity with the heart chakra. It is a useful crystal for those who wish to attract love, relax and enjoy life. It can help revive jaded relationships, recognizing unfulfilled needs and unspoken emotions. It attracts love to those who wear it, so it is recommended for those who feel neglected and unloved. Place morganite on the heart chakra to facilitate deep healing, especially with regard to traumatic relationships in your past.

Morganite can help reduce stress and treat stress-related problems. It is a profoundly relaxing stone that will soothe away all states of anxiety, so it is valuable for those who suffer from symptoms such as palpitations, panic attacks or hyperventilation. It is also useful for lung problems such as TB or asthma.

It is a wonderful meditation aid when it can help engulf the user in compassion and patience, prompting a more contemplative outlook on life.

OBSIDIAN

Classification: Mineraloid

Colour: Black

Hardness: 5.5

Lustre: Vitreous

Rarity: Common

Found: Mexico, Italy, USA, Scotland

Healing attributes: Grounding, scrying

Formed by the rapid cooling of volcanic lava, which chills so quickly that there is no time for crystals to form, obsidian has a glassy appearance and is a stone that is easily broken into sharp-edged pieces. One of the first minerals to be fashioned into tools by humankind, obsidian was used as spearheads and weapons from earliest times. When the Spanish conquistadors arrived in the New World in the 16th century, they were confronted by native peoples armed with obsidian-bladed knives and spears. The Aztecs and Mayans also employed obsidian for scrying to predict the future. Worn, tumbled obsidian pebbles are often called 'Apache tears', and spotted white 'snowflake obsidian' is formed by the addition of the mineral christobalite.

Obsidian is related to the base chakra and is an excellent grounding stone, making us feel stable and balanced. It represents eternal protection and will shield the owner from physical or psychic attacks. It helps purify a negative atmosphere and purges negativity from dysfunctional chakras and meridians. Obsidian can remove toxins from the body and from polluted sections of the Earth.

Highly polished balls of obsidian may be used for scrying; they not only predict the future, but also enable us to see into the 'shadow' sides of ourselves, furthering the awareness of self-knowledge. It can be a painful experience as we confront our deepest fears and pain. Obsidian ensures that it is a cathartic experience, however, bringing peace and light to the darkness.

OPAL

Classification: Silicate

Colour: Iridescent white, blue, green, fire (rainbow) black

Hardness: 5.5 –6

Lustre: Vitreous to pearly

Rarity: Relatively common

Found: Australia, Mexico, India, Slovakia, Peru, Britain

Healing attributes: Eyes, fevers

Known as opthalmios, or 'eye stone' to the Greeks, opals were reputed to improve the eyesight and the Romans called them opali, or 'seeing jewels'. Opals are not, strictly speaking, crystals, as they lack a molecular crystalline structure. Instead, tiny spheres of silicate and oxides, or hardened silica gel, reflect the light in a range of colours across the spectrum giving the stones their very attractive opalescence.

The Romans ranked opals second only to emerald in terms of value and desirability and regarded them as symbols of hope happiness and truth. The aboriginal people of Australia have a legend that the creator of the world came down to earth on a rainbow to spread his message of peace, and at the very spot where his foot touched the ground, the rocks became alive with sparkling colour, creating beautiful opals.

In healing, opals are aligned with the crown and brow chakras and will strengthen the life force. They can induce mystical dreams and enhance creativity and can be used for psychic protection. They can also help relieve fevers and the pain of childbirth. If used as an elixir, opals are also good for the eyes.

Opals have always been associated with love and passion (although interestingly, opal engagement rings are regarded as unlucky) and they encourage fidelity and loyalty in the wearer.

PERIDOT

Classification:	Silicate
Colour:	Yellowish-green to green
Hardness:	6.5–7
Lustre:	Vitreous
Rarity:	Uncommon
Found:	Red Sea, Myanmar, Pakistan, Arizona
Healing attributes:	Cleanses jealousy, revitalises the body

Peridot is the gem that is found in olivine, the olive-green peridotite rocks which make up the earth's mantle. Olivines are one of the most common minerals on earth, but they generally emerge only as tiny gems on the earth's crust. Peridots are much larger, far more rare and hence, highly valued gems. It has been mined and used as a gemstone for millennia. Reputedly Cleopatra's favourite stone, peridot was used by the ancient Egyptians for healing, and was probably one of the stones in the legendary breastplate of the Jewish high priest. Sometimes confused with emerald, and also known as chrysolite, peridot is distinguished by a paler and more yellow-green colour.

During the middle ages, it was believed that peridot could drive away evil spirits, and it is still used today to provide protection and to prevent others draining our energy. It is a revitalising and energising stone, which may be employed to banish lethargy, apathy and exhaustion and is a good overall tonic for the body.

Peridot has an affinity for the heart chakra and has the power to cleanse the heart of jealousy, resentment, bitterness and hatred. It enables us to forgive and forget, opening up the heart to joy and new relationships. It is a stone for releasing anger and guilt and is also excellent for detoxifying the liver and gallbladder. It also influences the eyesight, heals digestive complaints and fixes skin problems, especially warts.

PHENACITE

Classification:	Silicate
Colour:	Colourless, white, yellow, pink, brown
Hardness:	7.5–8
Lustre:	Vitreous
Rarity:	Fairly rare
Found:	USA. Brazil, Madagascar, Russia
Healing attributes:	Reinforces power of other crystals; spiritual healing

Phenacite (or phenakite) is a rare beryllium crystal that is frequently mistaken for quartz. The ancient Greeks called it phenakos, meaning 'deceiver', because of the common confusion over its identity.

It is a powerfully sensitive stone, with one of the highest vibrations of any crystal. The healing properties of phenacite depend to an extent on where the stone was mined; Brazilian phenacite almost instantly tunes in to the feminine wisdom of the angelic realms and Russian stones are especially effective in cleansing environmental energies.

Phenacite has an affinity for the crown and brow chakras, and if it is placed on the soul star chakra above the crown chakra, an immediate activation is evident. It is an excellent stone for meditation, allowing us to focus on our spiritual side and expanding our conscious knowledge of the mystical guides that protect us.

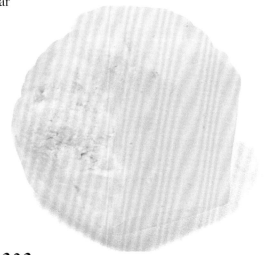

It can heal all levels of our being and when used with other stones in crystal therapy will reinforce the effectiveness of their healing powers.

QUARTZ

Classification:	Silicate
Colour:	Clear is most common, but also, smoky, rose, green, blue, tangerine
Hardness:	7
Lustre:	Vitreous or resinous
Rarity:	Most common mineral in earth's crust
Found:	Europe, Africa, North and South America
Healing attributes:	Useful on brow and crown chakras to cure headaches or toothache; can be programmed for any purpose and will amplify the effects of other crystals. Grounding (smoky quartz).

Quartz is the most abundant mineral on earth and occurs in a huge variety of rocks. Quartz crystals form six-sided prisms, terminating in six-sided pyramids. It is most commonly colourless and transparent (and known as rock crystal in this form), but there are many coloured varieties which are used as gemstones: amethyst, citrine (yellow quartz), rose quartz, milky quartz, smoky quartz (grey-brown), agate, chalcedony and jasper.

Quartz crystals have a natural frequency of vibration that varies according to the size and shape of the crystal. It is a very stable mineral and has the property of being piezoelectric – this means that when pressure is applied to a quartz crystal, a positive electrical charge is created at one end, and a negative one at the other. When an electrical current is passed across a quartz crystal, it vibrates slightly, and generates further pulses of electricity as it does so. When a crystal is introduced into an oscillating electrical circuit that resonates at a frequency close to that of the crystal, the whole circuit will adopt the crystal's natural frequency. Furthermore, the frequency will remain constant and regular over a long period of time. This is why quartz is used as an accurate timer in watches.

Legend has it that quartz crystals were used in the lost kingdom of Atlantis for rejuvenation, while ancient priests in a variety of cultures used it to destroy negative energies. The ancient Greeks believed that it was water that had been frozen by the gods, and called it krystallos, meaning ice. The Romans carried quartz crystals in the summer to keep their hands cool, and also used them to treat aches, pains, fevers and swellings. During the middle ages, quartz crystals were placed under the tongue to reduce fever. Clear quartz crystals were traditionally used to focus the sun's rays on parts of the body which needed healing.

Clear quartz

Clear quartz is used extensively in healing today and is known as the 'master healer'. Kirlian photography has revealed that when a quartz crystal is held in the hand, the strength of the energy field is at least doubled. So if you place a quartz crystal on any part of the body, you will increase the energy in that area. It is especially beneficial in healing headaches – rub a smooth, round crystal on the forehead to relieve the tension.Clear quartz can be used to stabilise any chakra and may be used on the crown chakra to bring clarity to meditation and dreams – it is worth remembering that crystal balls used for scrying are usually made from clear quartz. Clear quartz removes blockages in the chakras and revitalises the physical, mental emotional and spiritual planes, in addition to increasing energy fields. Healers recommend that everyone carry a piece of clear quartz for protection and to maintain balance; it is also useful to place a piece in your home or place of work.

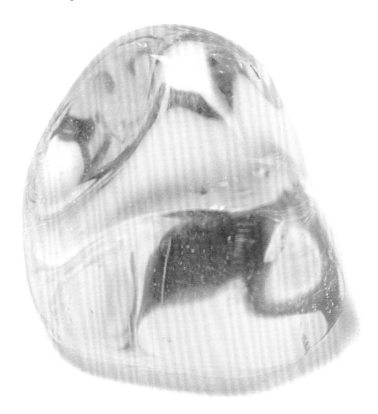

The various different hues of quartz incorporate further healing properties which relate to their colours.

Aqua aura quartz

Aqua aura crystals are artificially manufactured: clear quartz crystals are heated so that gold bonds with them to create a transparent aquamarine colour. Aquamarine is the colour of communication, so this crystal is used to stimulate the throat chakra. The combination of the most precious of metals with the clear crystal creates a powerful stone which will activate all the chakras, cleanse the aura and eliminate negativity, as well as boosting the immune system.

Rose quartz

Rose quartz is found in various shades of pink and has been used for centuries to heal the heart and treat fertility problems. In a related way, it is also known as the 'children's stone', because of its gentle powers. Especially effective for the heart chakra, this stone has the power to fill anyone with a sense of unconditional love for themselves, as well as for others. It enables us to give and receive love and to overcome emotional traumas by encouraging forgiveness. For those in search of love, rose quartz should be placed by the bed or in the relationship corner of a house in order to attract a relationship.

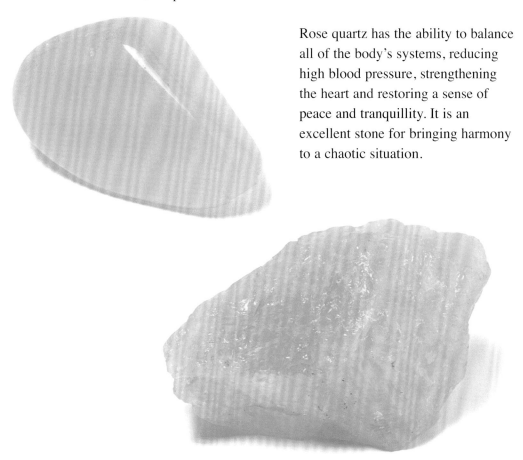

Rose quartz has the ability to balance all of the body's systems, reducing high blood pressure, strengthening the heart and restoring a sense of peace and tranquillity. It is an excellent stone for bringing harmony to a chaotic situation.

Green quartz

Green quartz opens, activates and balances the heart chakra, dissolving past hurts and resentments. It replaces negative emotions such as envy and bitterness with everlasting unconditional love.

Smoky quartz

The translucent colour of smoky quartz varies from light to dark brown-grey or black. It has an affinity for the solar plexus chakra and is an excellent grounding stone, which is often used at the end of a treatment session. Smoky quartz relieves stress and anxiety, calms a hyperactive mind, disperses fear, lifts depression and negativity, and encourages positives thoughts and action. Not surprisingly, soldiers traditionally carried a small stone of smoky quartz into battle as a talisman.

Smoky quartz is a detoxifying stone that aids elimination, especially of the digestive system. It can also protect against radiation and is a pain-relieving stone that alleviates back ache and eases muscular spasms.

Tangerine quartz

A light orange colour, tangerine quartz is associated with the sacral chakra, making is useful for sexual problems, including impotence, frigidity and fertility. It is also an excellent stone to employ following an injury or a trauma. It helps to restore energy to the area affected by the shock, and this vital power also make it useful in past life healing, where tangerine quartz uses its energies to harmonise past mistakes.

RHODOCHROSITE

Classification:	Calcite
Colour:	Rose pink
Hardness:	3.5–4
Lustre:	Vitreous to resinous
Rarity:	Common
Found:	England, Germany, Russia, South Africa, Japan, South America, USA
Healing attributes:	Heart chakra, cures depression

The rosy pink colour of rhodochrosite makes it instantly recognisable, and its name derives from the Greek rhodon, meaning rose, and chroma, meaning colour. It is one of the most important ores for manganese and often forms dramatic crystals in rock cavities. There are long rhodochrosite stalactites in the silver mines of the Incas in Argentina, which appear to hang like pink icicles and can be sliced open to reveal astonishing rings in different shades of pink.

Rhodochrosite is aligned with the heart chakra and on a physical level may help regulate the heart beat, stabilise the pulse, regulate blood pressure and stimulate the circulation. In emotional terms it will assist in lifting depression and encouraging a positive and cheerful attitude to life. It prompts spontaneity and is ideal for those who struggle to express their feelings. It is a stone of love and passion and some believe it has the power to attract one's soul mate.

It is a stimulating crystal that will energise the mind and encourage creativity and innovation. It also has the ability to alleviate migraines, skin disorders and thyroid imbalances, as well as kidney and intestinal problems.

RHODONITE

Classification: Silicate

Colour: Rosy pink to brownish red

Hardness: 5.5–6.5

Lustre: Vitreous to dull; pearly when polished

Rarity: Common

Found: Brazil, Mexico, Germany, Spain, Russia, Sweden

Healing attributes: Physical and emotional first aid

Like rhodochrosite, rhodonite gets its name from rhodo, the Greek for red. Unlike that mineral, however, rhodonite sometimes contains black streaks of manganese dioxide, giving the stone a dramatic colouring.

It is affiliated with heart chakra and is an excellent 'first aid stone' as it heals emotional trauma and can dispel panic attacks. It is a stone of compassion, allowing a flow of love to heal wounds caused by self-destructive or abusive behaviour. It encourages repressed feelings of bitterness, anger and depression to rise to the surface, to be released. As it is so effective in dispersing panic and anxiety it should be used as soon as possible after harrowing events to restore balance, calm and harmony.

On a physical level, rhodonite is effective in promoting healing in cuts, wounds and insect bites. It draws toxins such as pus to the surface for a rapid cure. It will also boost fertility, stimulate the libido and benefit disorders of the heart.

RUBY

Classification:	Oxide
Colour:	Red
Hardness:	9
Lustre:	Vitreous to adamantine
Rarity:	Widely available
Found:	Thailand, India, USA, Zimbabwe, Myanmar, Madagascar, Sri Lanka
Healing attributes:	Restores energy

An ancient stone that has been prized for thousands of years, rubies are well established in the folklore of cultures around the world. In the Bible in the Book of Job, the 'price of wisdom is above rubies', and in Proverbs, the value of a virtuous woman is 'far above rubies'. Ancient peoples believed that rubies were stones of the sun and directly linked to fire and the life force. Ruby is a variety of the stone corundum, the second-hardest mineral on Earth. Corundum is clear and the colour of ruby, which can vary from blood red to pale pink, is caused by traces of chromium within the mineral.

The colour of ruby exudes passion, and it is appropriate that ruby is the stone associated with 40 years of marriage – fitting testament to the enduring power of love. It is a stone of great energy and promotes a zest for life, although sensitive souls may find it a little overpowering. With its affinity for the base chakra, ruby will transform lethargy into liveliness, and eliminate apathy and exhaustion. It increases sexual activity so can also be used to treat frigidity and impotence. It stimulates the heart

chakra, filling the heart with joy, spontaneity, laughter and courage. It can instil great passion, confidence and lust for life.

Finally, as its blood red colour suggests, rubies are recommended for improving the circulation and quality of the blood.

SAPPHIRE

Classification: Oxide

Colour: Blue; also pink, purple, yellow, green, white, black

Hardness: 9

Lustre: Vitreous to adamantine

Rarity: Widely available

Found: Sri Lanka, Australia, Pakistan, India, Myanmar

Healing attributes: Detoxify, throat, wealth

Sapphire is another variety of the mineral corundum, and although the word sapphire is virtually synonymous with blue, sapphires are found in a range of colours from blue to green, indigo, pink, purple, yellow and white; sapphire actually refers to any non-red coloured corundum. The name is derived from the Sanskrit word sani, meaning Saturn, although the Greeks referred to it as sappheioros meaning blue. The deep blue of a sapphire is derived from the presence of titanium oxide within corundum, and different impurities produce the wide range of sapphire colours. The only one to have a distinct name is the rare orange-pink sapphire, which is known as padparadschah, named after the lotus blossom. Sapphires (and rubies) can be cut into exquisite jewels, and their colour can also be 'improved' by heat treatment, a practice that has been going on since at least Roman times, because Pliny mentions it in his Historia Naturalis, stating 'There is no fraud that yields greater profit than that of counterfeiting'.

The ancient Persians believed that the world rested on a giant sapphire, and that the sky was a reflection of its deep blue colour. Another legend stated that if a sapphire were put into a vessel containing a snake, the rays from the sapphire would kill it, so sapphires acquired a reputation as an antidote to snake venom.

Sapphire has always been associated with love, joy and fidelity, and is sometimes known as the 'wisdom stone'. Some sapphires are believed to be record-keepers and may provide access to ancient realms when dreaming or meditating. It can reduce spiritual confusion and bestow peace. In addition each colour of sapphire demonstrates a unique selection of healing properties.

Black sapphire is a stone for protection and grounding, which will boost self-confidence.

Blue sapphire has a particular affinity for the throat chakra and so encourages communication, promoting the expression of the truth. It is also useful for those engaged in public speaking and has physical benefits for the throat, thyroid and lungs. It has a calming and balancing effect on the nervous system and may be used as a meditation aid to open up the crown and brow chakras to the angelic realms.

Green sapphire helps to balance the heart chakra and boosts the immune system. It also promotes fidelity and loyalty.

Indigo sapphire activates the third eye chakra, enhancing psychic awareness.

Pink sapphire fills the heart with unconditional love and peace and will remove emotional blockages.

White sapphire enhances the crown chakra, establishing a close connection with the heavens and angelic spheres. It is a protective and powerful stone that will remove the obstacles to your spiritual journey.

Yellow sapphire balances and activates the solar plexus chakra, clearing the mind of negativity, stimulating the intellect and bringing wisdom. A detoxifying stone, yellow sapphire rids the body of impurities and stimulates the lymphatic system,. It is of particular value to the liver and gallbladder. Yellow sapphire is especially associated with wealth and prosperity, especially in the Far East, where it is identified with the Hindu god Ganesh, the remover of obstacles.

SELENITE

Classification:	Sulphate
Colour:	Clear, white, red, grey, brown, yellow
Hardness:	2
Lustre:	Vitreous to pearly
Rarity:	Common
Found:	Worldwide
Healing attributes:	Mediation, back problems

Selenite is a form of gypsum, an evaporite sulphate formed when salty water evaporates through rocks and soils, producing wonderful crystals. Selenite crystals can form long prismatic 'swords', most dramatically in the Cave of Swords in Chihuahua, Mexico, where some crystals are up to 2m (6ft) long. White selenite has been described as possessing a moon-like glow, and its name means 'moon rock', being derived from the Greek selene, for moon. A relatively soft mineral, selenite will gradually dissolve if left in water for an extended period.

Healers regard selenite has an excellent tool for meditation, as it allows access to both past and future lives and it is aligned with the crown chakra. Simply rub the stone while in the meditative state and take note of the images, visual symbols or feelings which fill your mind.

Selenite has a high vibration and is a wonderful stone for healing both physical and emotional ailments. Promoting flexibility of both mind and body (it is excellent for increasing the strength and suppleness of the spine), selenite encourages us to broaden our horizons.

Selenite provides protection against a variety of toxins, particularly the mercury amalgam in dental cavity fillings. It also has the power to stimulate cellular regeneration, so it will assist in healing wounds.

SHATTUCKITE

Classification:	Silicate
Colour:	Light to dark blue
Hardness:	3.5
Lustre:	Dull to vitreous
Rarity:	Rare
Found:	Arizona, USA
Healing attributes:	Intuition, tonsillitis/laryngitis

Shattuckite is a relatively rare mineral found almost exclusively in the Shattuck Copper Mine, Arizona, from which it got its name. The beautiful blue colour is produced by the presence of copper, and shattuckite is popular in both its polished or tumbled form.

It has an affinity for the throat and third eye chakras, and can alleviate throat conditions such as laryngitis and tonsillitis. It will also improve blood clotting. The elixir makes a useful tonic to revive and rebalance the body, especially in spring time.

Shattuckite is a powerful stone for channelling, enabling users to clearly verbalise the information being received from other worlds and it can assist in automatic writing. Shattuckite stimulates the third eye, enhancing intuition and clarifying psychic visions.

SUGILITE

Classification:	Silicate
Colour:	Purple
Hardness:	6.5
Lustre:	Vitreous to dull to waxy
Rarity:	Uncommon
Found:	South Africa, Japan, Canada
Healing attributes:	Grounding, pain relief

Sugilite is a rare and obscure mineral discovered in 1944 by the Japanese mineralogist Dr Ken-ichi Sugi, after whom the stone is named. Also known as luvulite, royal azel and New Age stone, sugilite's colour spectrum ranges from lavender to deep purple.

The stone's energy will flow from the crown to the base chakras and will improve self-confidence. It has an especial affinity for the brow and crown chakras and has the power to enhance the intuition and encourage the development of psychic abilities. It is a wonderful stone for meditation because it can connect to the pure love of the Divine.

It is a very useful stone for sensitive souls, those who feel that they are out of kilter with their surroundings. It enables us to understand why we are here and guides the user to the lessons that will teach them to value their lives. It is also a nurturing stone that helps us to confront unpleasant situations and fears, encouraging us to accept what we must face.

Sugilite is also a superb pain-reliever and can be placed on the forehead to dispel headaches.

SUNSTONE

Classification:	Silicate
Colour:	White, yellow, orange
Hardness:	6–6.5
Lustre:	Vitreous to dull
Rarity:	Uncommon
Found:	Sri Lanka, USA, Canada, Russia
Healing attributes:	Restores optimism, leg pain

Olgigoclase is by no means a well known mineral, but the semi-precious version, sunstone, is a popular crystal. Usually a pale yellow shade, sunstone sometimes exhibits flashes of reddish colour from the traces of haematite within the stone. It was used in Native American rituals and placed in the middle of the medicine wheel, where it is said to glow. In India it was used to provide protection against enemies.

Yellow sunstone is allied to the solar plexus chakra and removes stress and fear by suffusing the energy centre with light. An uplifting crystal, sunstone will revitalise the user, filling them with love, and laughter, boosting self-esteem and optimism. In crystal therapy, sunstone is used for treating eating disorders and to encourage weight loss.

It is also regarded as a bringer of luck and can be used by athletes to treat cartilage problems or painful legs.

TANZANITE

Classification: Silicate

Colour: Indigo blue

Hardness: 6.5–7

Lustre: Vitreous

Rarity: Uncommon

Found: Tanzania

Healing attributes: Spinal disorders, psychic protection

Tanzanite is mined in one place – the hilltop at Merelani, ten miles south of Tanzania's Kilimanjaro airport – and when excavated, it has a dull green colour. Tanzanite is heat-treated to achieve the lavender-blue colours so popular with gem dealers. Indeed, soon after its discovery in 1967, tanzanite was marketed heavily by Tiffany's the jewellers and it has since become one of the most fashionable gemstones in the world. Tanzanite is a variety of the mineral zoisite, but Tiffany's suggested a name change, because, they said, 'blue zoisite' sounded uncannily like 'suicide'!

Tanzanite is a spiritual stone that is aligned with the brow and crown chakras. A stone of transformation, it can dissolve old patterns of disease and karma, enabling us to move forward with optimism and focus. It endows us with a sense of direction, allowing us to use our powers for the highest good.

It enhances healing at all levels and protects the healers themselves. Physically it clears the throat and lungs and relieves disorders of the skin, ears and eyes. It boosts the immune system and is recommended for speeding recovery after an illness as it regenerates cells and tissues. Tanzanite is also useful in treating spinal problems.

THULITE

Classification:	Silicate
Colour:	Reddish
Hardness:	6
Lustre:	Vitreous
Rarity:	Common
Found:	Norway, Austria, Australia, USA
Healing attributes:	Sexual problems, breathing difficulties

Thulite is another form of the mineral zoiste and is an opaque pinkish stone that derives its colour from manganese. It was first discovered in Lom, Norway in 1821 and was named after the mythical island Thule which is described in Greek and Norse legends. Pinkish thule is particularly therapeutic, but it also occurs as green, yellow or grey varieties.

Thulite is particularly recommended for use with the heart, third eye, and sacral chakras. By helping to activate the heart chakra, it enables the expression of unconditional love and is outstanding for those who have experienced hurtful relationships. It bestows energy and strength on the wearer and provides a sense of adventure.

Physically, thulite may be used to treat heart disease and breathing disorders such as asthma. It is also beneficial for the reproductive organs and can be used to alleviate sexual problems and enhance the libido as well as fertility.

225

TIGER'S EYE

Classification:	Silicate
Colour:	Blue, brown, red, black
Hardness:	7
Lustre:	Silky
Rarity:	Common
Found:	South Africa, USA, Mexico, India, Australia
Healing attributes:	Courage, mental clarity

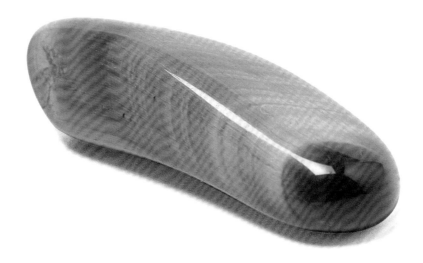

Tiger's eye is a form of quartz, an opaque, chatoyant gemstone in which the vertical fibrous inclusions in the stone reflects the light in a cat's eye' effect. Tiger's eye is usually polished and cut en cabouchon to enhance this effect. It is usually golden-brown, but may also be red, blue or black. Roman soldiers used to carry tiger's eye because they believed it provided protection in battle, and during the middle ages tiger's eye was worn to ward off the evil eye and repel witchcraft.

Tiger's eye has a particular affinity for the solar plexus chakra as its golden brown hues bring together the energies of heaven and earth, lifting our vibrations, while at the same time providing feelings of stability.

It is a stone which will enhance mental clarity, allowing us to see a problem objectively, unclouded by emotions. Use it in times of confusion to help clarify your goals and make the right decisions.

Recommended as a protective stone, tiger's eye dispels fear and anxiety and will counteract feelings of hypochondria, making it an excellent stone for those prone to psychosomatic illness. With its ability to increase willpower, focus, courage and self-confidence, it additionally balances mood swings and releases tension.

Tiger's eye is also useful in the treatment of neck and throat disorders, eye problems and reproductive illnesses, as well as strengthening the spinal column, releasing toxins and alleviating pain.

TOPAZ

Classification:	Silicate
Colour:	Yellow, colourless, blue, greenish, pink
Hardness:	8
Lustre:	Vitreous to adamantine
Rarity:	Uncommon
Found:	Brazil, Pakistan, USA, Russia, Mexico
Healing attributes:	Confidence, digestion

An ancient precious stone, with a range of beautiful pale colours, topaz may have acquired its name from the Sanskrit word tapaz, meaning fire; alternatively it may derive from the legendary isle of Topazios in the Red Sea (now called Zebirger) which was the source of topaz in Roman times. Given the right conditions, topaz can grow into enormous crystals, with one specimen weighting 100kg (220lb). The ancient Egyptians believed that topaz was coloured with the rays of the sun god Ra, and regarded it was a powerful amulet. Similarly, the Romans associated it with Jupiter, their god of the sun, and the ancient Greeks believed it was a 'stone of strength' that could make the wearer invisible in times of crisis. African bushmen use topaz in their ceremonies to communicate with the spirit world and to attract wealth and health.

Topaz is a stone of vitality that is aligned with the abdomen and solar plexus chakras. It can speed up a sluggish metabolism and stimulate the meridians. It can be used to treat eating disorders such as loss of appetite, bulimia, anorexia and obesity.

It eliminates feelings of doubt and uncertainty, magnifying self-confidence. Topaz is an excellent stone for attraction and manifestation: it will attract people to you on both social and business levels. It enables you to manifest your desires, as long as they are for the greater good. It is a stone that promotes honesty and is an admirable emotional support.

TOURMALINE

Classification:	Silicate
Colour:	Colourless, every colour in the spectrum
Hardness:	7.5
Lustre:	Vitreous
Rarity:	Common
Found:	Sri Lanka, Afghanistan, Brazil, Africa, USA, Australia, Italy
Healing attributes:	See individual colours

Tourmaline is actually the name for a group of closely related minerals: they are borosilicates transformed by minute traces of chemicals which give a range of over 100 different colours. Some crystals even exhibit more than one colour: watermelon tourmaline, for example is pink and green. Known as the 'rainbow gemstone', tourmaline's name comes from the Sri Lankan (or Sinhalese) tur mali, meaning multi-coloured stone. Like clear quartz, it is piezoelectric, meaning that it acquires a small electrical charge when heated or rubbed.

Tourmaline was widely used by shamans and can be a useful scrying stone. It is a stone which enhances self-knowledge and will transform mental negativity into a positive outlook. Individual colours of tourmaline have their own healing properties.

Black tourmaline, or schori is a superb grounding stone for use after a
treatment. It is also effective if you are feeling 'spaced out'. It offers powerful protection against the negative energy emitted by other individuals or from the spiritual plane. If used with mica, black tourmaline will reflect it, sending the bad vibes back to the sender. It also deflects negative energy from electrical equipment and neutralises the effects of radiation. An energy-enhancer that increases feelings of vitality and well-being, this stone may be used to treat lower back problems and adrenal disorders.

231

Blue tourmaline (indicolite) activates the throat and third eye chakras and will heal disorders of the throat, lungs and eyes. An important stone for improving communication, blue tourmaline also facilitates the release of suppressed grief. In physical terms, it is effective in cooling and healing burns.

Green tourmaline (verdelite) fills the heart chakra with love and compassion and will encourage emotional issues to rise to the surface so they can be released, cleansing individuals of past-life traumas. It balances the emotions and dissolves stress and fear, which in turn induces tranquillity and improves sleep patterns. A revitalising stone, it will help those suffering from exhaustion, may calm hyperactive children, and finally, will encourage healthy plant growth.

Pink tourmaline is often given as a token of love or friendship, reflecting its affinity with the heart chakra. It can also act as an aphrodisiac. It is a stone which has the power to comfort and can provide solace to the recently bereaved. In healing, it may be used to treat the heart, lungs and skin.

Yellow tourmaline

(elbaite) activates the solar plexus chakra, stimulating creativity and the intellect, bestowing clarity of mind and increasing feelings of courage and personal power. It is an excellent crystal for those in business. In healing, it may be used to treat the liver, kidneys and stomach.

TURQUOISE

Classification: Phosphate

Colour: Turquoise

Hardness: 5–6

Lustre: Dull to waxy

Rarity: Common

Found: Turkey, Iran, Afghanistan, USA, Mexico, Australia

Healing attributes: Depression

The amazing colour of turquoise is caused by the presence of copper and aluminium in the mineral. It is a gem that has been treasured for thousands of years: it was mined in the Sinai peninsula by the ancient Egyptians, although for generations the best turquoise came from Persia, where it was worn as a talisman for good fortune. Native Americans also valued it, believing it promoted healing and good luck. The Navajo produced exquisite jewellery and carvings and apparently believed that it was a piece of sky that had fallen to earth. It was brought to western Europe by the crusaders and the name may come from the French for Turkish, reinforcing the belief that it came f rom Turkey.

The vibrant colour of turquoise makes it an excellent stone for treating depression. Healers have used it to calm minds in turmoil following a nervous breakdown, and to prevent panic attacks. It can be used to balance all the chakras, although is especially associated with the throat, heart and brow chakras.

Turquoise may be worn to protect against negative energies and pollution. It is said to change colour to warn of danger or illness (although the physical properties of turquoise make it sensitive to external influences such as skin pH, so they might fade over time anyway).

It has many uses, including pain relief and alleviating muscular and skeletal complaints, as well as relieving digestive problems, high blood pressure, fevers, asthma and inflamed eyes.

INDEX

CREDITS

My deepest love and gratitude to my dear husband, Garry and children, Chloe and Thomas, for their patience and inspiration. Thanks also to Steve at Earthworks, who so patiently gave of his time.

The author and publishers would also like to thank the models, Martin Amo and Caron Bosler.